世遗之城：泉州

QUANZHOU: A WORLD HERITAGE CITY

流风遗韵——宋元泉州非遗的承与传

A Living Legacy: Intangible Cultural Heritage of Quanzhou Since Song-Yuan Period

中共泉州市委宣传部 编

海峡出版发行集团 | 福建人民出版社
THE STRAITS PUBLISHING & DISTRIBUTING GROUP | FUJIAN PEOPLE'S PUBLISHING HOUSE

目 录

Contents

引　言

2021 年 7 月 25 日，“泉州：宋元中国的世界海洋商贸中心”赫然跻身《世界遗产名录》，更多世人拜服于她窖藏千年的文化富矿，渴饮世代传承的文化原浆。于是，一座名唤“刺桐”的光明之城，不再踽踽于粗粝的岁月，而是尽力伸展其本就博大的身姿，用愈加超然的心境，鸣奏世纪鼓点，起舞丝路长风。

世遗之城泉州，恰如新出浴之美人。如何小心翼翼地保护这绝代风华，让一座宝藏城市，熨帖又精准地赓续其“半城烟火半城仙”的多元包容传统，以及“见人、见物、见生活”的活态传承特征？

按照《世界文化遗产申报工作规程》，开展基础研究、价值研究和比较分析，提炼出具有说服力的杰出普遍价值是申报世界文化遗产的必备条件。此前，泉州申遗文本编制时，专家即建议挖掘提炼闽南文化核心价值，强调泉州非遗对世界文化遗产价值、功能、地位、传播的支撑。

大美泉州，似有藏天下于一州之势。目前，泉州共有 600 多个县级非物质文化遗产代表性项目，其中，被列为市级代表性项目的有 262 个，省级代表性项目 128 个，国家级代表性项目 36 个，还有 6 个被联合国教科文组织列为人类非物质文化遗产代表性项目，可谓天花板级别，令人望尘莫及！

多姿多彩的非物质文化遗产，正是对泉州世遗价值的生动佐证和有力支撑，如对土木结构遗产点保护与修缮真实性、完整性提供支撑的闽南传统民居营造技艺、泉州木雕等，对桥梁、码头及其他石结构遗产点价值、功能提供支撑的惠安石雕、洛阳桥传说、姑嫂塔传说等，对具有管理、生产、运输、交易、消费、服务功能遗产点提供支撑的南音、南戏、五祖拳、送王船、通远王信俗、蟳埔女习俗、嗦啰嗹习俗、德化窑与磁灶窑烧制技艺、永春香制作技艺、水密隔舱福船制造技艺等。

善护美，是一种态度，更是一种信仰；远方再远，有了美，也足以以文化之。今天的泉州正着力打造世界遗产保护利用典范城市和全国最具烟火气的旅游目的地，以系统保护、活态传承、活化利用展示世遗之城风姿，非物质文化遗产，是其中浓墨重彩的一笔，也是沟通泉州与世界最好的桥梁之一。

Introduction

On July 25, 2021, "Quanzhou: Emporium of the World in Song-Yuan China" was inscribed into the *World Heritage List*. Lauded as the "City of Light" by the renowned Italian explorer, Marco Polo, Quanzhou was known also as "Zayton" in ancient times. With the revival of the Maritime Silk Road, "the spirit of inclusiveness and common prosperity, embodied by the ancient city, runs in a similar vein with the country's current pursuit of a shared future for all" and the city is embracing a new opportunity.

While a new chapter is unfolding in Quanzhou, the safeguarding of its diverse, open and inclusive cultural tradition, as well as the inheritance and transmission of its living heritage, has become an important theme.

In accordance with the *Procedures for the Declaration of World Cultural Heritage* issued by the National Cultural Heritage Administration of China, Outstanding Universal Value (OUV) extracted from basic research, value research and comparative analysis is a prerequisite for the application of UNESCO's World Cultural Heritage. Previously, when the text for world heritage application of Quanzhou was being prepared, experts suggested that the core values of Minnan (Southern Fujian) culture should be explored and refined, and that the support of Quanzhou's intangible cultural heritage to the value, function, status and dissemination of world cultural heritage should be emphasized.

Quanzhou is unparalleled in terms of the number of intangible cultural heritage items dotted around the whole city. Among its 600 or more heritage items, 6 are included in UNESCO's *Representative List of the Intangible Cultural Heritage of Humanity*, 36 are of national level, 128 are of provincial level and 262 are municipal ones.

The colorful intangible cultural heritage is the vivid evidence and strong support for the value of Quanzhou as a world heritage site. The architectural craftsmanship of traditional residence in Minnan and Quanzhou wood carvings are testimonies to the authenticity and integrity of the protection and renovation of civil structure heritage sites. Hui'an stone carvings, tales about Luoyang Bridge and the Sisters-in-Law Pagoda demonstrate the value and function of such heritage as bridges, docks and other stone structures. Nanyin Music, southern operas, Wuzuquan, the Ong Chun ceremony, the belief in King Tongyuan, the custom of Xunpu women, the ritual of Anhai Suo Luo Lian, the porcelain firing techniques of Dehua and Cizao kilns, the producing techniques of Yongchun incense and the watertight-bulkhead technology of Chinese junks are striking examples to support heritage sites with the functions of management, production, transportation, trading, consumption and service.

Quanzhou is now striving to build a model city for the protection and use of world heritage and the country's most cozy and homely tourist destination with effective protection and promotion of its living heritage. The serial items of intangible cultural heritage and the spirit they embody is definitely one of its highlights as well as one of the best links and bridges between the city and the world.

传承中的泉州非物质文化遗产。（陈英杰 / 林劲峰 / 陈小阳 摄）
Quanzhou intangible cultural heritage in conservation and transmission. (Photo by Chen Yingjie, Lin Jinfeng and Chen Xiaoyang)

民间文学：
古港潮起潮落，海风娓娓述说

Folklore of Quanzhou

陈三五娘传说：千山暮雪闯情关，泉潮缔结荔镜缘

Tale of the Mirror and the Lichee (Chensan and Wuniang)

姑嫂塔传说：面海已有一千载，情若当初下南洋

Tale of the Sisters-in-Law Pagoda

洛阳桥传说：万古安澜，闽中桥梁甲天下

Tale of Luoyang Bridge

陈三五娘传说：
千山暮雪闯情关，泉潮缔结荔镜缘

“问世间，情是何物，直教生死相许？”爱情作为人类生活中极为重要的事，自古就被誉为自然繁衍的“造化之基”，社会教育的“王化之端”。古今中外，它一直是各类文艺作品的永恒主题。

在闽南文化中，也有一个以追求真爱为主题的经典传说家喻户晓。它就是《陈三五娘》。

《陈三五娘》始于民间传说，后来演化为戏曲，戏曲故事又使前者更富有传奇色彩。学者们似乎更愿意从其丰富浪漫、曲折生动的故事情节去揣摩，这大概是一代代闽南人的集体创作。

梨园戏《陈三五娘》演出剧照。（陈智勇 摄）
A stage photo of *Tale of the Mirror and the Lichee* performed in Liyuan Opera. (Photo by Chen Zhiyong)

相传在一个元宵夜，潮州名媛黄五娘携婢女益春睇灯，恰逢路过此地的泉州才子陈三也在赏灯，二人有了一见钟情的开始。此时五娘与陈三虽同生爱慕，却只能以礼自持，各奔东西。一日，五娘对着窗外艳丽的桃花挥毫，和陈三诗一首，恰被伶俐的丫鬟益春撞破心事，于是娇羞佯斥。与此同时，恶少林大对五娘念念不忘，威逼利诱，让五娘之父同意将五娘许婚。五娘见林大为人鄙俗，痛彻心扉，反而倍思陈三。

Tale of the Mirror and the Lichee (Chensan and Wuniang)

As a very important part of human life, romantic love has always been the eternal theme of all kinds of literary works at all times and in all countries.

The pursuit of true love being its theme, *Tale of the Mirror and the Lichee* is a household tale in Minnan (Southern Fujian) district.

Started as a folktale, *Tale of the Mirror and the Lichee,* known more widely as *Chensan and Wuniang* in Chinese, was adapted into an opera, which, as the collective creation of the literati in Minnan district, makes it all the more romantic with the dramatic twists and turns of the plot.

Legend has it that during the Lantern Festival on the 15th of the first lunar month, whilst enjoying the lanterns, Wuniang, the fifth daughter of a rich Chaozhou family, accompanied by her maid, Yichun, met a young scholar, Chensan, from Quanzhou. The two fell in love at first sight, but it was a brief encounter as Chen went on his way to send off his brother to take up an official position in the neighboring province. Later, Wuniang's feelings for Chen was perceived by her maid when she pinned her lovesickness on a picture of peach blossoms with a poem. Lin, the eldest son of a local rich man also saw Wuniang in the lantern show and was hung up on her, so he made her father agree to his proposal of marriage by trickery and coercion. Sick of Lin's vulgarity, Wuniang fell into deep sorrow and missed Chen all the more.

而陈三完成家事后，立即重返潮州追寻意中人。是日，陈三自楼下经过，不意与五娘重逢。五娘喜不自胜，以绣帕裹荔枝抛掷。陈三计上心来，装成磨镜青年，故意失手碎镜，卖身入黄府。一日，黄父外出，益春帮助陈三上楼与五娘相会，两人互吐衷肠。陈三得知黄父迫女成婚，五娘抗拒，甚至欲以身殉情，深为感动，遂与五娘誓共生死，相约出走。是晚三更，陈三携五娘、益春夜奔故乡泉州。

不同于中国四大民间传说中的爱情悲剧，《陈三五娘》最闪耀的地方就在于敢于反抗封建礼教，敢以“人的文学”为宗旨，尊重爱情，尊重人性，最终达成一个完美的结局。鲁迅说，悲剧就是把美好的东西打碎给人看。而《陈三五娘》却启发听者：“所爱隔山海，山海皆可平！”它非要让爱情的力量去打破命运的桎梏，这恰恰符合现代人的爱情理念，可谓从古老的文明中荡漾出最真挚的人性光辉。

从某种集体潜意识来看，它的诞生与风行可以说是一种文学史的暗合与投契，即闽南民众对中国最古老的文学经典——《诗经》的伟大致敬。君不见，《诗经》开篇即歌颂纯洁美好又缠绵悱恻的爱情：“关关雎鸠，在河之洲……”

爱情这条河流，从《诗经》流淌到《陈三五娘》，逶迤到今天，不舍昼夜。

His job done, Chensan immediately returned to Chaozhou seeking his Miss Right. One day, Chen saw Wuniang unexpectedly while walking past her house and the latter was beside herself with joy, so she threw some lichees wrapped in her handkerchief from upstairs to show her own feelings. Chen was so excited that he came up with an idea to go to Wuniang's house by disguising himself as a mirror polisher and after breaking the treasure mirror, he sold himself to Wuniang's family as a servant to compensate for the mirror. One day, when Wuniang's father went out, Wuniang's maid arranged a tryst for the two lovers. Chen was deeply moved when he learned that Wuniang disagreed with his father's arranged marriage and wanted to kill herself for love. He vowed to share life and death with Wuniang and they decided to elope. At midnight, Chen took Wuniang and her maid out and left for his hometown, Quanzhou.

Different from the four classic tragedies of love in Chinese folklore, namely, *The Butterfly Lovers: Liang Shanbo and Zhu Yingtai*, *Tale of the White Snake*, *Lady Mengjiang* and *The Cowherd and the Weaver Maid*, the

许书纪老人讲述《陈三五娘》传说。（洛江区文旅局 供图）
Mr. Xu Shuji narrates the tale about Chensan and Wuniang. (Courtesy of Tourism Bureau of Luojiang District, Quanzhou City)

best part of *Tale of the Mirror and the Lichee* lies in its bravery to rebel against feudal ethics, to write with humanitarianism and individualism as the ideological basis, to show respect for love and human nature, and thereby comes up with a happy ending. Lu Xun, the famous Chinese writer, once put it that tragedy is to destroy all the pretty things for people to see, whereas the message we get from *Tale of the Mirror and the Lichee* is that true love conquers all, which is just on par with the modern notion of love and reflects there was respect for human nature in our ancient classics.

The birth and popularity of *Tale of the Mirror and the Lichee* is the collective wisdom of the literati in Southern Fujian and the tribute they pay to *The Book of Songs*, the earliest anthology of Chinese poetry, which begins with praises of pure, beautiful and sentimental love.

Be it the earliest classics like *The Book of Songs* or *Tale of the Mirror and the Lichee*, romantic love is the ever-lasting theme.

姑嫂塔传说：
面海已有一千载，情若当初下南洋

“每当夕阳西沉的时候，我总是在这里盼望你。天空中虽然飘着雨，我依然等待你的归期……”当我们听到这首《外面的世界》，感叹它生动表达了企盼爱人回归的愁绪时，很多人并不知道，早在400多年前，已有一位资深史学家何乔远在福建写下了《闽书》，而书中记载的一个动人故事，就像歌曲中所唱的那样，扣人心弦，悱恻缠绵：“昔有姑嫂嫁为商人妇。商贩海，久不至，姑嫂塔而望之，若望夫石然，塔中刻二女像……”

姑嫂塔传说凄美动人。很久以前，泉州府城南门外的石狮宝盖山下有姑嫂二人，哥哥为生活所迫，南渡出洋谋生，约定三年后坐船归来。姑嫂二人天天登上宝盖山山巅，垒石垫脚，翘首远眺大海归舟，盼望亲人回家团聚。终于三年时间过去，哥哥乘船回来，姑嫂俩在山上看到船已近海岸，谁知忽然刮起狂风、下起暴雨，惊涛骇浪把船打翻了。哥哥葬身大海，姑嫂俩喜尽悲来，双双纵身跃入大海……人们为了纪念她们，就建起了这座姑嫂塔。

姑嫂塔全貌。（郑文桂 摄）
A panorama of the Sisters-in-Law Pagoda. (Photo by Zheng Wengui)

姑嫂塔又名关锁塔。关于这座塔，《泉州府志》记述：“关锁水口镇塔也，高出云表，登之可望商舶来往。”姑嫂塔始建于南宋绍兴年间，据史料记载，正是从那时候起，泉州的先民大量移居菲律宾及南洋各地。《泉州府志》载，从北宋崇宁元年（1102）到清乾隆二十三年（1758）的 656 年中，泉州发生大旱 11 次，造成了“民多饿死”“民多游移”等悲惨情景。乡民大量远涉重洋，背井离乡到南洋谋生。何乔远在其《镜山全集》中写道：“（华侨）皆背离其室家，或十余年未返者，返则儿子长育至不相识。盖有新婚之别，娶以数日离者。”

Tale of the Sisters-in-Law Pagoda

While in many songs we find the melancholy moments of longing for the return of the beloved, not many people know that as early as some 400 years ago, there was a story echoing these in *The Book of Min* (finished in 1620) written by He Qiaoyuan (1558—1632), a noted historian in local history as well as a native of Quanzhou.

The story about the Sisters-in-Law Pagoda is a very sad one. Long long ago, there lived at the foot of Baogai Hill, some 20 kilometers southeast of the city of Quanzhou, a couple and the younger sister of the husband. Necessity obliged the man to sail to Southeast Asia to seek his fortune and he promised to return in three years. His wife and his younger sister missed him so much that they crested Baogai Hill to wait for him every day. They piled up stones on the top of the hill to stand higher and see farther for his boat. Three years later, the man returned in a boat. But when he was about to go ashore, a sudden storm sank the boat. Witnessing the death of their loved one, the wife and the younger sister were so despaired that they jumped into the sea. Later, people built the Sisters-in-Law Pagoda in memory of them.

According to the records in *Local Chronicles of Quanzhou Prefecture*, during the 656 years from 1102 to 1758, Quanzhou was hit by 11 droughts, which resulted in the starvation and emigration of many people. Many people in Quanzhou were forced to leave for Southeast Asia in the hope of scraping a living. First built during the Southern Song Dynasty (1127—1279), the Sisters-in-Law Pagoda witnessed the emigration of many of the ancestors of Quanzhou to Southeast Asian countries like the Philippines. It was also named Guansuo Pagoda (pagoda to lock up the wind and water) as the usual practice of the Chinese to bring happiness and wellbeing, which is known as "Fengshui". Ascending the hill to where the pagoda piercing the skyline, one could see merchant ships coming and going.

姑嫂望夫的传说因此应运而生。泉州从事航海经商的人，都将此塔视为故乡的象征。史料记载：“华侨出，每见塔影沉海，即知离乡远去，无不潸然落泪。逢返梓，则喜登舱远眺，见姑嫂塔浮于海面，知故乡将近，则无限欢欣。”爱乡怀土的闽南人也把“关锁烟霞”誉为“古泉州十景”之一，姑嫂塔则成为古代泉州港重要的航标。

姑嫂塔传说丰富的人文价值可与巫峡神女峰、涂山望夫石相较。作为涉侨民间文学作品中的一枚瑰宝，其思想内容和海外侨胞的情感相通，因此在海内外有着广泛影响。而故事的流传也使得姑嫂塔成为凝聚“番客”乡愁的精神载体，成为海外侨亲精神家园的航标。同时，姑嫂塔传说也是侨乡人民心目中一段特殊的历史文化记忆。每到农历正月，人们纷纷扶老携幼，上宝盖山，登姑嫂塔，遐思那一段凄美的传说。

望海处，思悠悠。化为涛，不回头。

As is documented in the collected works of He Qiaoyuan, hard life forced many overseas Chinese, some of whom were newlywed husbands, away from their native land to seek a living abroad, and when they returned after some ten years, their own children couldn't even recognize them.

It was under this context that came the story of the Sisters-in-Law Pagoda The pagoda was a symbol of the hometown for those Quanzhou maritime merchants. They knew they were far away from home when the pagoda was out of sight, while when the pagoda came into view, they knew they would be home soon. A signal tower as well as an important navigation mark in the ancient time, the Sisters-in-Law Pagoda was hailed as one of the "Top Ten Views of Ancient Quanzhou" by the home-loving people of Quanzhou.

The story of the pagoda is not only attractive but also of wide appeal both home and abroad as it is folk literature related to overseas Chinese in its own right. It records the unique history and becomes the spiritual symbol for oversea Chinese from Quanzhou. The pagoda is a mecca for locals every first lunar month when people celebrate the Spring Festival. They climb the mountain and ascend the pagoda for a panoramic view.

Many years have passed, yet the sea is still surging, and the story of the Sisters-in-Law Pagoda has been passed on.

烟锁塔影。（李群育 摄）
The Sisters-in-Law Pagoda wrapped in mist. (Photo by Li Qunyu)

洛阳桥传说：
万古安澜，闽中桥梁甲天下

“嬴氏曾驱六合人，蔡侯只用一州民。立犀岂不贤川守，鞭石何须役海神。”

这是宋人刘克庄咏叹泉州洛阳桥的诗句。

关于洛阳桥，泉州人似乎有太多的话要说。数百年来，这座荣膺“海内第一桥”桂冠的跨海梁式大石桥，无论是其桥基营造的独特性（筏形基础），还是堪称神来之笔的“种蛎固基法”，都足以让人惊叹不已。更何况，它的意义早已超越了物理形态，成为乡愁文化和人格坐标的表征。

面对它，中国著名桥梁专家茅以升教授赞叹道：“在我国古桥中，神话传说最多、几乎举国皆知的，北方有赵州桥，南方有洛阳桥。”

洛阳桥桥头历朝历代石碑林立。（陈英杰 摄）

There are stone tablets from different dynasties standing at the end of Luoyang Bridge. (Photo by Chen Yingjie)

Tale of Luoyang Bridge

The construction of Luoyang Bridge, as is recorded in a work of the Song Dynasty (960—1279) poet, Liu Kezhuang, was supervised by Cai Xiang, the magistrate of Quanzhou and it united the efforts of local government and the people of Quanzhou.

The significance of Luoyang Bridge has long gone beyond a mere wonder of architecture. It has become a spiritual and cultural symbol. Luoyang Bridge is praiseworthy in many ways. As the first stone beam bridge built across the sea in ancient China in the middle of the 11th century, how it was built is still a wonder even to this day. First is its raft-shaped foundation, namely, casting a great number of stones along the major axis of the bridge to form a stone dike which connected the river bottom, on which piers were built to reduce erosion due to tidal and river flows. Second, consolidating the foundation of the bridge by raising fast-breeding oysters so as to take advantage of their strong adhesive force.

As the famous Chinese bridge expert, Mao Yisheng, acclaimed, among the bridges known throughout China, the two that abound in the largest number of myths and legends are Zhaozhou Bridge in the north of China and Luoyang Bridge in the south.

洛阳桥位于今泉州台商投资区洛阳镇和洛江区万安街道交界处的洛阳江入海口，原名万安桥，寄寓“万古安澜”之意。作为世界桥梁筏形基础的开端，洛阳桥已被列为全国重点文物保护单位。它始建于北宋皇祐五年（1053），与卢沟桥、赵州桥、广济桥并称为“中国四大古桥”。北宋至和二年至嘉祐五年（1055—1060），蔡襄两次出任泉州太守，相传他在任期间主持洛阳桥建造工程，呕心沥血，有口皆碑。史载，此桥营建工期前后历七年之久，耗银一千四百万两。建桥九百余年以来，先后修复十七次。由于洛阳桥建造在江海交汇处，江阔水深，工程艰巨，衍生了许多与之有关的民间故事，如蔡襄母亲渡江发愿、蔡太守移檄海龙王、八仙襄助建桥、蔡襄请九日山海神镇海造桥等，大都将营造洛阳桥之功归于蔡襄，细节编排出神入化。

同时，洛阳江两岸优美的风光不但为文人雅士提供了赋咏的题材，也成为民间百姓寄托美好愿望之所在，洛阳桥连日月潭、清源洞通洛阳江、李五重修洛阳桥、方太守洛阳江祷雨等故事也因此家喻户晓。许多以蔡襄和洛阳桥为素材的民间传说从不同的角度反映了洛阳江两岸的山川风貌及蔡襄等历史人物的事迹，歌颂了劳动人民的传统美德与聪明才智。千百年以来，这些传说广泛流传于泉州、台湾地区及东南亚一带的华侨华人中间。

泉州民谚曰：“做人应当‘站如东西塔，卧似洛阳桥’。”从这个意义出发，这座桥的精神内涵对于闽南文化无异于一种家训。该桥取名“洛阳”，也源于泉州人不忘开基之祖来自中原河洛的寻根情怀，而“甲天下”的盛誉，从来不在于石墩的厚重、岁月的悠长，而是那份乡愁的分量。

洛阳桥永远慰藉着酾酒临江的浪子心，一如泉州籍诗人余光中晚年所咏叹：

刺桐花开了多少个四月
东西塔依旧矗立不倒
江水东流，海波倒灌
多少人走过了洛阳桥

Previously named Wan'an Bridge (forever peace and safety), it is located across Luoyang River at the junction of Quanzhou Taiwan Investment Zone and Luojiang District. As the first bridge built with a raft-shaped foundation, it is listed as a major historical and cultural site protected at the national level. First built in 1053 during the Northern Song Dynasty, it is one of the four most famous ancient bridges in China. The other three are Guangji Bridge in Guangdong Province, Zhaozhou Bridge in Hebei Province and Lugou Bridge in Beijing. It is said that, from 1055 to 1060, Cai Xiang had served as the magistrate of Quanzhou twice and he supervised the construction of the bridge. And it is recorded that it took 7 years and cost 14 million *liang*, about $ 6 million, to built the bridge. And over the past 900 years, the bridge has been repaired 17 times. As the bridge was built at the estuary where the tides and rapids were swift, the project was formidable and people credited Cai Xiang for the completion of the bridge and hence inspired a great many folktales about his efforts and the difficulties he experienced in the process.

The beautiful scenery along Luojiang River also provides a wealth of stories. From those folktales and legends that are still popular in Quanzhou, Taiwan and Southeast Asia, we can get a glimpse of the landscape along Luojiang River, know about deeds of historical figures like Cai Xiang and learn traditional virtues from the working people and their intelligence and creativity.

As a popular Quanzhou proverb goes, a man should stand like the East and West Pagodas in Kaiyuan Temple and sleep like Luoyang Bridge, meaning we should always stay true to ourselves, being righteous, virtuous and generous. The spiritual connotation of this bridge is some kind of a family motto. People in Quanzhou named the bridge "Luoyang" in homage to their ancestors from He-Luo area centered with Luoyang City. The reputation "No. 1 Bridge in the World" the bridge enjoys lies not only in the massiveness of its stone piers and long history, but also in the strong surges of nostalgia.

As was mentioned in the poem by the famous poet Yu Guangzhong, a native of Quanzhou, Luoyang Bridge and the East and West Pagodas in Quanzhou have always been the emotional sustenance of travelers far away from home.

洛阳桥风光。（张九强 摄）
A fine view of Luoyang Bridge. (Photo by Zhang Jiuqiang)

传统表演艺术：
刺桐丝竹绕远帆，宋元南戏在梨园

Traditional Performing Arts

泉州南音：横抱琵琶执节歌，千家罗绮管弦鸣

Quanzhou Nanyin Music

泉州北管：江淮盐兵携来，小调买舟过海

Quanzhou Beiguan Music

泉州拍胸舞：东方迪斯科，疑是闽越风

Quanzhou Chest-Slapping Dance

泉州木偶戏：一根悬丝贯五行，一口布袋多出戏

Quanzhou Puppetry

梨园戏：老戏泉腔，当年七了搬演

Liyuan Opera (Pear Garden Theater)

高甲戏：角分九色，丑行亦挑大梁

Gaojia Opera

打城戏：融贯佛道法事，打通天堂地狱

Dacheng Opera

泉州南音：
横抱琵琶执节歌，千家罗绮管弦鸣

老泉州人念叨的古早文化，始终不离“拳头、烧酒、曲”。其中的“曲”，便是泉州南音，亦称弦管，是经联合国教科文组织评定的人类非物质文化遗产代表作。虽然史书和典籍缺乏完整的记载，但音乐学界从古乐名称、演奏形式、乐器遗制、曲目内涵和记谱方法等反溯历史，公认泉州南音是“中国音乐历史的活化石”。关于南音，著名音乐学家田青曾经如是评说：“直到听到了泉州南音，我才敢下这样的断语——古老的中国音乐，真的一直流传到了今天。”

溯源音乐史不难发现，弦管是魏晋时对丝竹音乐的通称，五代后蜀也都以弦管描述乐事。聆听南音，就是一次去往古典中国的穿越之旅。你看它的演奏形式，右琵琶、三弦，左洞箫、二弦（宋称奚琴），执拍板者居中而歌，俨然“丝竹更相和、执节者歌”的汉代相和歌遗制，令识鉴者不免恍然惊呼：此阵势不就是南唐《韩熙载夜宴图》的现场版吗？

都说音乐是流动的建筑，殊不知，建筑也是音乐现场的指认者。寻宝泉州，细心的你不但能领略各弦管班社的世代传承、复制，还能在开元寺大雄宝殿和甘露戒坛的飞天乐伎手中发现各种宋代的弦管乐器。文化遗产之间的互证有时竟可这般神妙。

泉州开元寺甘露戒坛的飞天手持宋代弦管乐器。（陈英杰 摄）
Flying Apsaras with stringed and piped instruments of the Song Dynasty can be found in the Sweet Dew Altar of Precepts of Kaiyuan Temple in Quanzhou. (Photo by Chen Yingjie)

Quanzhou Nanyin Music

Southern Shaolin Martial Arts, alcohol drinking and music are three inseparable parts in the lives of people in Quanzhou, among which music refers to Nanyin Music, or stringed music which is included in UNESCO's Representative List of the Intangible Cultural Heritage of Humanity. Although there's no complete records in historical books and classics, it is generally acknowledged in the music circle that Nanyin Music is "a living fossil of ancient Chinese music" in terms of the name, the performance form, the making of musical instruments, the content of music and the system of notation. The famous musician, Tian Qing, so commented, "It's not until I heard Nanyin Music in Quanzhou that I came to the conclusion that the ancient Chinese music really has been handed down and remains popular till today."

Nanyin Music is also known as *Xianguan* (string and pipe music), a term people used to refer to music during the Wei-Jin (220—420) and Later Shu (934—965) periods. Listening to Nanyin Music is to take a journey back to ancient China. With a person holding the clapper and singing in the middle, a balloon guitar called *pipa* and a three-stringed guitar called *sanxian* on the right, and a bamboo flute called *dongxiao* and a two-stringed guitar called *erxian* on the left, its performance is just in line with that of Xianghe Song, a form of ancient songs from the Han Dynasty（206 B.C.—220 A.D.), characterized by the harmonious blending of stringed and piped instruments. Connoisseurs enjoying the performance cannot but marvel, "Isn't this the live version of the figure painting *The Night Revels of Han Xizai* by the Southern Tang (937—975) artist Gu Hongzhong?"

It is said that music is liquid architecture, whereas architecture is the identifier of music as well. It takes an observant eye to explore the city of Quanzhou. A sharp-eyed tourist, while enjoying different kinds of music, will also find the Song Dynasty musical instruments of Nanyin Music held in the hands of those Flying Apsaras in the main hall and the hall behind called the Sweet Dew Altar of Precepts in Kaiyuan Temple. How cultural heritages are connected and echo one another is a real miracle.

再看看南音独特的记谱方法。南音“工乂谱”自成体系，以“乂工六思一”五个谱字对应“宫商角徵羽”，同时附有琵琶指法和撩拍符号。有人将其误读为“工尺谱”，其实它比敦煌古谱还要缜密。现已发现南音“指套”“大谱”和“散曲”两千多首（套），在古乐之林中蔚为大观。那些悠长缓慢的大撩曲珍存着古代西域音乐文化的某些信息，延续着汉唐以来华夏音乐的血脉。自宫廷、教坊和贵族之家逐步流向民间，与民间音乐结合之后，其悠长缓慢的特色依然存在。有人认为这反映了农耕时代的悠闲自得，也有人认为这是它致命的短板，断言“老听众没了，南音就会消亡”，但事实是它们顽强地存活在南音弦友“腹内”，代代相传。一位女作家感叹，南音流传下来了，原汁原味，慢得如此彻底，慢成全世界之最，慢成联合国教科文组织的人类非物质文化遗产代表作，慢成精神贵族的奢侈品，尤其在这个追崇“秒杀”的新时代。

南音弦友知多少？六千万人的闽南文化圈里，没有人不知晓南音。有大海的地方就有南音，南音萦绕在闽南红砖古厝里，又跨越波涛汹涌的大海，走台湾，下南洋。赵朴初先生在听过南音之后，留下这样的诗句：“管弦和雅听南音，唐宋渊源大可寻。不意友声来海外，喜逢佳节又逢亲。”

一种活态的历史，总有着隐秘的传承谱系。南音的原乡泉州更是一派别样的风流：凡俗的市井百姓，早已淡定地在皇恩浩荡的御赐凉伞下，横抱一面琵琶，竖吹一管洞箫，执节歌吟出“御前清客”遥远的绝响。而谁，又在那弦管和鸣中，听出了一个时代的前世今生？

传承非遗，泉州少儿艺术团南音表演。（张九强 摄）
The performance of Nanyin Music by Quanzhou Children's Art Troupe, inheritors of the intangible cultural heritage. (Photo by Zhang Jiuqiang)

The uniqueness of Nanyin Music also lies in its system of notation. Nanyin has it own notation system called Gongchepu, often misread as Gongchipu, which has five scales, namely, Che, Gong, Liu, Si, Yi, corresponding to Gong, Shang, Jue, Zhi, Yu (Do, Re, Mi, Sol, La), the five basic scales of Chinese ancient music originated from the Spring and Autumn Period (770—476 B.C.). Meanwhile, it also has its own fingerings for pipa (balloon guitar) and signs for the clapper. This system of notation is even more detailed and complicated than those of Dunhuang Music. It is more than impressive that Nanyin, as an ancient music, boasts more than 2,000 repertoires surviving until now. Nanyin can be tracked back to the Han and Tang dynasties. Combining various music elements, including music from some Western Regions, royal palace music which court musicians migrating south as a consequence of civil wars brought and local folk music, it has slow and lingering melody. Some hold it that the music reflects a bygone age when the pace of life was unhurried, while others maintain that this is exactly its fatal defect and assert that, "With audience of the older generation gone, Nanyin will sink into oblivion." But in fact, with the devotion and commitment of players and fans of Nanyin, the music is passed down through generations. A woman writer marveled at the fact that Nanyin should survive in this quick-fix society and that it is so well-preserved that as a spiritual enjoyment, it made its way to UNESCO's Representative List of the Intangible Cultural Heritage of Humanity.

Popular among the 60 million people of Minnan origin, Nanyin not only lingers in the ancient red brick houses of Southern Fujian, but also spreads to areas like Taiwan and some Southeast Asian countries. Zhao Puchu, calligrapher, poet and former president of the Buddhist Association of China so commented on Nanyin in his poem, "One would always marvel at how well Nanyin retains the features of the culture of the Tang and Song dynasties. And during a joyful festival as such, it's a blessing to have friends and relatives from far and wide gather together to enjoy the music."

A living history always has its own knack of spreading and inheriting. In Quanzhou, home to Nanyin, the music once could only be heard in the palace has long been a common enjoyment for everyday people. Isn't it amazing?

穿越时光的泉州南音表演现场。（陈英杰 摄）
A trip back through time with the live performance of Quanzhou Nanyin Music. (Photo by Chen Yingjie)

泉州北管：
江淮盐兵携来，小调买舟过海

艺术没有疆界，天南地北的基因融合往往带来意想不到的天籁绝音。一个多世纪以前，多元包容的泉州文化中诞生了一个新的乐种——北管。

它原是江淮一带的民间音乐，自清光绪初年通过海上运输、盐兵南下和淮河决堤所致难民迁徙等传入泉州惠北（今泉港区），受方言影响并融入泉州、莆仙的特色音乐，形成独具泉港地方特色的新乐种。

20 世纪 20 年代后期至 50 年代初期，峰尾、后龙、山腰等地有 50 多个北管教习馆，著名的有升平社、清平社、金兰社、丽泽社和金兰明义社，几乎每个村落都有北管乐队，活跃于民间庆典、普度、迎神、装阁、出游、朝拜等活动。北管还伴随华侨、港澳台同胞远渡重洋，中国台湾和东南亚一些地区也有北管乐社。

因表演方式不同，泉州北管分为曲和谱两大类，有 223 首曲谱，其中声乐曲 57 首，器乐谱 166 首。曲大多数源于明清以来的江淮小调，谱大多数源于广东音乐、江南丝竹和京剧曲牌。北管演唱时采用官话（湖广话，相当于现代的普通话），在曲的前奏和乐句、乐段结束处演唱者经常边唱边执打击乐器伴奏。谱演奏时一般不用锣鼓，只用板或木鱼鼓打强拍。

泉州泉港黄素石楼前的北管演奏。（陈英杰 摄）
Beiguan Music performed in front of the stone-earthen building of the Huang Su family in Quangang District of Quanzhou. (Photo by Chen Yingjie)

Quanzhou Beiguan Music

Art knows no boundaries. The fusion of musical elements from different parts of the world often produces unexpected heavenly sounds. More than a century ago, a new genre of music, Beiguan, was born in the diverse and inclusive culture of Quanzhou.

Originally a folk music from the Yangtze-Huaihe Region, it was introduced to Huibei, Quanzhou (today's Quangang District) through sea transport, the southward movement of salt squads (local armed forces that investigated the private smuggling of salt in the Qing Dynasty) and refugees from the flood-stricken areas along Huaihe River during the early years of the Guangxu Period (1875—1908) in the Qing Dynasty. Influenced by the local dialect and incorporated into it the musical elements of Quanzhou and Puxian (today's Putian), it later developed into a new genre of music with unique distinctive characteristics of Quangang District.

From the late 1920s to the early 1950s, in towns and streets of Quangang District, such as Fengwei, Houlong and Shanyao, there were some 50 or more Beiguan-Music clubs, among which the most famous ones were Shengping Club, Qingping Club, Jinlan Club, Lize Club and Jinlanmingyi Club. Almost every village in Quangang District had its own Beiguan-Music band which was inseparable in many events such as folk celebrations, festivals, ritual rites, weddings, ritual parades and pilgrimages. It was also spread to areas like Taiwan, Hongkong and Macao, and even to overseas countries. Today, Beiguan-Music clubs can still be found in Taiwan and some Southeast Asian regions.

Among the 223 repertoires of Beiguan, 57 are vocal pieces and 166 are instrumental scores. Most of the vocal pieces originate from music of the Yangtze-Huaihe Region during the Ming and Qing dynasties (1368—1840), and they are sung in the official language, Huguang dialect (equivalent to modern Mandarin), and there are always accompaniments of percussion instruments at the prelude and the end of a phrase or a passage. The instrumental scores derive mainly from Cantonese music, stringed and wind music from the South of the Yangtze River and Beijing Opera, and they are usually played without gongs or drums. Only clappers and wooden fish drums are used for the strong beat.

从唱奏的艺术特色和风格看，北管可分为南、北两大流派。南派，即今泉港区山腰街道、前黄镇、涂岭镇、山腰盐场的北管乐队，以山腰北管乐团最具代表性。这里的方言偏重于闽南腔，人们比较习惯欣赏南音、芗剧等，乐队中常配有小唢呐、琵琶等闽南十音常用的乐器，艺人唱奏北管的同时，不知不觉地融入南音、芗剧的唱奏方法和风格，音乐高亢有力，色彩较为明快；北派，即今泉港区峰尾镇、后龙镇、南埔镇、界山镇的北管乐队，这些地方的方言多为头北话（闽南语系与莆仙语系过渡方言），人们习惯欣赏莆仙戏曲和音乐，乐队中常配有伬胡、双清等莆仙十音常用的乐器，艺人唱奏北管时揉入莆仙音乐风格特点，音乐纯朴柔和，色彩较为暗淡。

泉州北管的音乐风格既保留江淮一带民歌的明朗优雅，又融入闽南、莆仙音乐的柔婉秀丽，形成遒劲、朴实的个性，素有“天子传音”的誉称。

大泉州的文明，一如它的江河港汊，纵横交错，星罗棋布。北管是一道诗意的暗河，穿过幽暗的时光隧道，曾自北向南，逶迤而来；结缘经典，它又将满载一曲曲笙歌，轻敲哪些识鉴者的耳畔？

庆典游行队伍中的北管乐队。（陈英杰 摄）
A Beiguan-Music band performing in a celebration parade. (Photo by Chen Yingjie)

In terms of the artistic characteristics and style of singing and playing, Beiguan Music can be divided into two schools, the southern and the northern. The southern school, best represented by Shanyao Beiguan-Music Band, is made up of bands from Shanyao Street, Qianhuang Town, Tuling Town and Shanyao Saltwork in Quangang District. People there speak Minnan dialect and are partial to Nanyin Music and Xiangju Opera (also Gezai Opera), which are usually integrated into the performances of Beiguan Music, and together with *xiaosuona* (the Chinese Oboe), *pipa* (balloon guitar) and the other commonly used musical instruments in the music of Southern Fujian, making them loud, powerful and lively. Whereas the north school consists of bands from Fengwei Town, Houlong Town, Nanpu Town and Jieshan Town where people speak Toubei dialect (a transitional dialect between Minnan dialect and Puxian dialect) and have a preference for Puxian Opera and music which are often integrated into the performances, and together with the octagonal lute called *shuangqing*, the two-stringed fiddle called *chihu* and other commonly used musical instruments in the music of Puxian, making them low, deep and soft.

Beiguan Music of Quanzhou has blended the brightness and elegance of folk songs from the Yangtze-Huaihe Region and the softness and beauty of music from Southern Fujian and Puxian to form its unique, vigorous and simple style. It is also known as "Music of the Son of Heaven", for legend has it that the Jade Emperor, the supreme ruler of heaven, once sent two princes to earth to guide the practice of Beiguan bands.

Beiguan Music, the integration of music from the north and the south, adds to the appeal of Quanzhou culture.

泉州拍胸舞：
东方迪斯科，疑是闽越风

他们用七个节拍征服你，赤手空拳，应节合拍；他们不打别人专打自己，拳拳到肉，嗨翻全场。仔细一瞅，才知这群微醺的汉子，在跳一种大道至简的原始舞蹈。他们膂力过人，通体红透，仿佛要拍遍周天362个穴位，打通奇经八脉，使得浑身上下三万个毛孔无一处不舒张，获得通天彻地的清爽。

人们称之为泉州拍胸舞，它是福建最有代表性的民间舞蹈之一。长期以来，这种舞蹈主要流行于泉州市鲤城区浮桥、江南等社区。拍胸舞者多为健硕男子，头戴草箍，赤裸上身及双足，双掌合击之后依次拍打胸、肘、腿等部位，使之发出响亮的声音，并以此作为舞蹈之节奏，使原始粗犷的舞蹈有了后来被称为“七拍”的节奏。

泉州拍胸舞表演。（陈英杰 摄）
A performance of Quanzhou Chest-Slapping Dance. (Photo by Chen Yingjie)

Quanzhou Chest-Slapping Dance

Drawing the audience's eyes with just seven beats, the performers dance to the beats barehanded and barefooted. They slap not others but themselves on the flesh and bring the house down. To take a closer look, you'll see a group of men a bit tipsy dancing a simple and primitive dance. With surprisingly great strength, they slap their whole bodies red, as if they want to tap on all of the 362 acupuncture points of human body, unblock tendons and collaterals and open up the thirty thousand pores to have they themselves totally refreshed.

People in Quanzhou called it the Chest-Slapping Dance and it is one of the most representative folk dances in Fujian Province. It's been popular in communities in Fuqiao Street and Jiangnan Street in Quanzhou's Licheng District. Chest-slapping dancers are mostly strong men, wearing straw hoops on their heads, shirtless and barefooted. After clapping their hands, they slap their chests, elbows and legs in turn to make loud sounds as the beats of their dance, which give this primitive and rough dance a rhythm later called "seven claps".

神采飞扬的拍胸舞舞者。（陈起拓 摄）
The spirited chest-slapping dancers. (Photo by Chen Qituo)

据研究，古代八闽大地气候湿热，蛇类大量繁殖，古闽越人学会了与蛇共处，并由此形成了独特的蛇图腾崇拜。在重要的祭祀场合，他们会隆重地在舞蹈者头上箍上前端向上翘起三四寸的草箍，草绳随着舞者的动作而灵动摇曳，犹如吐着红信的蛇头，充分表达了蛇崇拜的内涵。更有史料表明，东汉许慎在《说文解字》中称，“闽”字门内有虫，此虫即为蛇。由此可知拍胸舞渊源之古早。

唐代以后，泉州成为中国四大对外通商口岸之一，繁荣的经济和包容的城市性格使得多种文化宗教、歌舞戏曲在泉州兴盛，而这也成为拍胸舞长期留存、生生不息的社会原因。地方戏曲也融入了拍胸舞元素，脍炙人口的梨园戏《李亚仙》就是其典型例证。在过去很长一段时间里，慎终追远的泉州人每逢白事，必请一拍胸舞队到场，以求祛灾纳吉，而那热闹的氛围，多少也有些事死如生的意味。为了生活，乞讨度日之人也沿街拍胸取悦施主，故拍胸舞也有过“乞丐舞”之别称。这一切，都成为拍胸舞传承的沃壤。

总之，这是比广场舞更喜乐、比迪斯科更律动的节拍舞，它热烈奔放，刚柔并济。其舞姿、队形、表情、神态，构成了一套十分有韵味的表演体系。表演者顾盼之间神采飞扬，那带着生命力和灵魂震撼力的节拍以及奔放到极致的表现力原始浓烈，遒劲洒脱，呈现出了不被工业文明驯化的原生态，恰似“行走的荷尔蒙”。

每逢传统民俗表演活动，拍胸舞总能将气氛推向高潮。（林劲峰 摄）
Chest-Slapping Dance never fails to take the spotlight whenever there are events for traditional folk performances. (Photo by Lin Jinfeng)

According to some studies, the climate of ancient Fujian was hot and humid and snakes proliferated. But Minyue people, the indigenous ethnic group living here during the Qin and Han dynasties (221 B.C.—220 A.D.) learned to coexist with snakes and thus formed a unique snake totem worship. On important ceremonial occasions, they would solemnly put on the dancers' heads straw hoops with the front ends turning ten to thirteen centimeters upward. And the straw hoops swayed with the movements of the dancers as if snakes were sticking out their tongues and thereby conveyed the message of snake worship. According to the explanation in *Origin of Chinese Characters*, the oldest comprehensive Chinese character dictionary compiled between 100 and 121 A.D. during the Eastern Han Dynasty by Xu Shen, in " 闽 ", the Chinese character for Fujian Province, there is a radical standing for the snake inside; hence we know that the Chest-Slapping Dance could be traced back to the ancient times.

After the Tang Dynasty (618—907), Quanzhou became one of the four major international trade ports in China. The booming economy and the inclusive society made it possible for various cultures, religions, songs, dances and operas to prosper in Quanzhou. And this is also the reason for the long-term survival of the Chest-Slapping Dance. Some local operas have integrated in them elements of the dance, a typical case of which is the widely loved piece in Liyuan Opera titled *Li Yaxian* (also *A Scholar and a Courtesan*). It has long been a custom for the people in Quanzhou to invite a chest-slapping dance team to perform in funerals so as to dispel the disaster and invite good luck. And the liveliness somehow suggests Quanzhou people's attitude to treat the dead as if they were alive. Besides, some people begging for a living perform the Chest-Slapping Dance in return for the kindness of their donors, and that's why it is also nicknamed "the Beggar's Dance". All these make it possible for the Chest-Slapping Dance to be passed down.

Sometimes high-spirited and intense yet sometimes soothing and pleasant, the Chest-Slapping Dance is more joyful than square dance and more rhythmic than disco. The posture, formation, expression and manner make the performance very appealing. The great energy as shown by the performers, the powerful beats, and the bold and unrestrained movements all present to the audience a picture of the primitive vitality of human life.

泉州木偶戏：
一根悬丝贯五行，一口布袋多出戏

也许是泉州先贤的禀赋给予木偶戏太多的哲理，那些不甘于被造物主拨弄命运的时刻，都化为股掌之间的一条丝线、一口布袋。

小小的木偶，你以为它在演戏，那么你错了，它说的是人生；你以为它说的是人生，那么你又错了，它只是在演戏。

泉州木偶戏主要有两类，一类是南派布袋戏，另一类是提线木偶戏。

南派布袋戏指的是泉州地区的掌中木偶戏，它以泉腔（即南曲）演唱戏文，以区别于唱北调的漳州北派布袋戏，闽南民间称之为“掌中傀儡”“手套式木偶”，其班社称“掌中班”。

掌中木偶戏被称为“布袋戏”的缘由主要有两点：一是掌中偶人的形象构造必须有个布内套，以之连缀头部及四肢，外面套戏服，演员的手掌也是在布内套中活动，巧妙地为偶人做各种身段动作；二是掌中班的全部行头用一口袋子就能装下，不用戏箱，便于流动演出。

提线木偶和掌中木偶。（陈英杰 摄）
The glove-puppet show and the marionette theater. (Photo by Chen Yingjie)

Quanzhou Puppetry

One string or one glove alone can be used to manipulate the movements of a puppet. It's the aspiration of the ancestors of Quanzhou to hold destiny in their own hands that gives birth to Quanzhou Puppetry.

If you think the little puppet is just acting, you are wrong. It's presenting a life story to you. While if you think it is telling a life story, you are wrong again. It is just acting.

Quanzhou Puppetry can be divided into two schools, namely the southern school of glove-puppet shows and the marionette theater.

Generally known as "the show in the palm", the southern school of glove-puppet shows refers to the shows performed in Quanzhou, which are sung with Nanyin Music so as to distinguish themselves from the northern school of glove-puppet shows in Zhangzhou, a neighboring city.

Glove-puppet shows are nicknamed "cloth-bag shows" for two reasons: first, besides the costumes, every puppet has a cloth inner lining which is sewn to the head and the limbs of it and resembles a glove for a performer to enter his fingers to control the movements of the puppet; and second, the costumes and props are so portable that for the touring troupe, a cloth bag instead of a trunk is enough to pack them all.

南方布袋戏历史悠久，东晋王嘉《拾遗记》载：“南陲之南，有扶娄之国，其人善机巧变化……或于掌中备百戏之乐，宛转屈曲于指间。”说的就是一种指掌技艺，与后世“指头傀儡”相似。泉州至迟在五代时就已有掌中傀儡演出。明中叶至清末是闽南布袋戏演出的兴盛时期，出现了许多著名艺人，如李克茶（破涧茶）、同安梭、黄琴、黄华等，其中李克茶于道光末年创办了金永成布袋戏班，与同安梭等五位艺人被观众誉为“六才子”。

提线木偶戏古称“悬丝傀儡”“线戏”“木人戏”等，闽南语系地区称之为“傀儡戏”“嘉礼戏”。其源头与远古巫文化关系甚密。提线木偶戏本为丧家乐，汉代成为宾婚嘉会中“贯彼五行、超诸百戏”的独特表演艺术，晋唐时随中原士族南迁入闽。

宋元时期，泉州成为“东方第一大港”，社会经济十分发达，多元文化交汇共荣，寺庙林立，祈福禳灾、酬神还愿、醮事出煞等民间信仰与民俗活动极为繁盛。泉州傀儡戏充分发挥其巫文化潜质和“沟通人神”的独特功能，与道教等宗教的科仪活动紧密结合，成为民众生、老、病、死等生命礼俗中不可或缺的部分。

泉州木偶戏表演。（陈英杰 摄）
A Quanzhou marionette show. (Photo by Chen Yingjie)

Glove-puppet shows enjoy a very long history and the earliest record of them can probably be found in the ancient book titled *Records of Picked-up Leftovers*, a collection of supernatural stories compiled by Wang Jia of the Eastern Jin Period (317—420). Recorded in the book are people in the southern borderland who were so ingenious and dexterous that they invented some small figures that could present shows in human palms. This is similar to today's glove-puppet shows which appeared in Quanzhou in the Five Dynasties (907—960) at the latest. Puppet shows of Quanzhou were in their heyday from the middle of the Ming Dynasty (1368—1644) to the late Qing Dynasty (1636—1912), a period during which many puppeteer masters emerged, such as Li Kecha, Tong'an Suo, Huang Qin and Huang Hua, among whom Li, founded Jinyongcheng Puppet Troupe, the first of its kind in China and he himself was hailed as one of the six most talented puppeteers of the time.

Quanzhou marionette was called "string puppet", "string show" or "wooden man show" in the ancient time and was also referred to as "kuilei xi" or "jiali xi" in Minnan dialect. Its origin is closely related to the ancient *wu* (witch) culture. The puppet show was originally a funeral music, but in the Han Dynasty, it became a unique performing art in wedding ceremonies and gatherings and was introduced into Fujian Province with the southward migration of the imperial clan during the Jin and Tang dynasties (266—907).

During the Song and Yuan dynasties (960—1368), Quanzhou became "the largest port in the East" with well-developed economy and a rich mix of cultures. There were many temples, folk beliefs and folk activities such as praying for good fortune, rewarding the gods and sacrificial rituals. Working closely with Taoism and other religions in various ritual activities, Quanzhou marionette, as a unique witchcraft that helped with the communication between people and gods, became an integral part of the rituals of life, including birth, old age, illness and death.

由于泉州傀儡戏表演技艺独特精湛且颇具文学性，可“雅俗共赏”，因而也深受士大夫、文人的喜爱。宋南外宗正司皇族子弟习此艺者甚众，常“提傀儡娱宾”。明代泉州傀儡戏班社林立，演出兴盛，与宋元南戏诸艺种长期交流融合，演出剧目、音乐唱腔、表演技艺、偶像造型工艺等已成熟完备，成为宋元南戏重要分支泉腔戏曲的组成部分，且已形成科班传习制度。

今天，泉州木偶戏表演艺术颇受世界瞩目。“福建木偶戏后继人才培养计划”于2012年成功入选联合国教科文组织《保护非物质文化遗产优秀实践名册》，成为全球十项优秀实践名册项目之一，也实现了中国在该名册上零的突破。

戏里戏外，都是人生。一条丝线，一口布袋，像极了人生的纵贯线与小天地。列位看官，当我们在戏耍傀儡之时，焉知傀儡不是在戏耍你？

木偶戏表演《钟馗醉酒》。（林劲峰 摄）
Drunken Zhong Kui, the Demon Hunter, a traditional marionette show. (Photo by Lin Jinfeng)

The unique and exquisite performance and its aesthetic value made Quanzhou marionette theater appealing to all ages and social groups. In the Song Dynasty, many descendants of the imperial clan who moved to Quanzhou learned puppetry and often entertained their guests by playing a part in marionette shows. The exchanges and integration with different genres of music during the Song and Yuan dynasties made Quanzhou marionette theater an important and mature branch of Quanzhou operas, which had its own repertoire, singing style, performance skills, puppet crafting as well as training system. In the Ming Dynasty (1368—1644), there were numerous marionette troupes and their shows were very popular.

Today, the performing arts of puppetry in Quanzhou are attracting worldwide attention. In 2012, the "Strategy for the Training of Coming Generations of Fujian Puppetry Practitioners" was successfully selected as one of the ten projects on UNESCO's *Register of Good Practices for Safeguarding Intangible Cultural Heritage*. It's a breakthrough for China to enter the list.

A piece of string together with a cloth bag presents to us a whole world of life, and yet, "All the world's a stage, and all the men and women merely players. They have their exits and their entrances."

泉州木偶剧团演员走进幼儿园，与师生一起表演木偶戏。（陈英杰 摄）
The artists of Quanzhou Marionette Troupe came to a kindergarten and performed a puppet show with the teachers and children. (Photo by Chen Yingjie)

梨园戏：
老戏泉腔，当年七子搬演

自唐玄宗开梨园之后，从事戏曲业的优伶们便以梨园为招牌，但敢以“梨园戏”冠名的剧种，天下只此一家。于是，有人戏称：“看戏不看南戏，到底是不懂戏。南戏不看梨园，终究是心头恨。”

梨园戏肇始于唐五代时泉州的歌舞百戏技艺，是宋元南戏的遗存剧种，被学术界誉为“古南戏的活化石”。植根于历史文化名城泉州，它较完整地保存了古典戏曲的诸多剧作与演出形态。

梨园戏分为“下南班”“上路班”和贵族府第的“家班”，三者各以不同的看家戏“十八棚头”互相竞胜。下南班与上路班均以成年人组班，各自可以“优人互凑”，故合称“大梨园”，俗称“老戏”；家班由童伶组成，又名“小梨园”“七子班”，俗呼“戏仔”。从现存剧目看，梨园戏保留的传统剧目有 70 余部，多为宋元戏文，其中尚存南戏轶篇、海内孤本。其音乐为曲牌连缀体，以箫弦伴奏为主，一字多腔，用泉音演唱；打击乐则以南鼓（压脚鼓）为主，打法独特，风格古朴。表演形式更是严整规范，有“举手到目眉，分手到肚脐，拱手到下颌”等基本动作构成的“十八步科母”，与敦煌壁画中人物的手姿有着一脉相承、异曲同工之妙。总之，这是一种精致独到的戏曲典范，从戏棚、乐器到服饰、道具，都精致到无以复加。

梨园戏表演。（张九强 摄）
A performance of Liyuan Opera. (Photo by Zhang Jiuqiang)

Liyuan Opera (Pear Garden Theater)

Ever since Emperor Xuanzong of the Tang Dynasty set up in Liyuan, his pear garden, the first royal acting and musical academy in China, actors and actresses who engaged in the profession started to use "Liyuan" to refer to themselves. However, there is only one opera in the world that dare to take the title of Liyuan Opera. Hence, someone observed half-jokingly, "A theatergoer who has never seen operas in southern China is not a real buff. While, if he says he has, and yet, it's not Liyuan Opera, it's a huge pity."

Derived from the various performing arts of Quanzhou during the Tang and Five Dynasties period, Liyuan Opera is acclaimed as "the living fossil of ancient Southern Opera" as it preserves a large repertoire of Southern Opera from the Song and Yuan dynasties. Rooted in the historical and cultural city of Quanzhou, it has completely preserved many plays and performances of Chinese classical operas.

Liyuan Opera is categorized into three schools, "xianan ban", "shanglu ban" and "jia ban", each of which has its own stock repertoire of "Shiba Pengtou" (eighteen traditional basic programs). Xianan and shanglu are of the Big Liyuan school (adult troupes), for members of the two schools are adults who are irregularly employed, while jia ban (junior troupes) is known as Small Liyuan or the seven-member troupes as they were originally private opera troupes and the members are children. Among Liyuan Opera's 70 or more stock repertoires, most are traditional libretti and scores of Southern Opera from the Song and Yuan period. Being the only copies extant, some pieces are very rare. Liyuan Opera is exquisite and unique, either from the stage to instruments or from costumes to props. Sung in Quanzhou dialect and accompanied by flutes, stringed instruments and the southern drum (foot-pressed drum), its music is a medley of set tunes and there are various keys for the same lyric. As for the performance, Liyuan Opera has very strict formulaic staging rules, known as the "eighteen fundamental steps" which lay great emphasis on hand movements that are rich, delicate and unique. Surprisingly, the gestures resemble those of the figures seen on the murals of Dunhuang Grottoes.

1949 年后，国家和文化界有识之士大力抢救、挖掘、传承梨园戏传统剧目、音乐唱腔、表演艺术等，使其作为一种传统文化遗产得到保护。进入新时代，梨园戏艺术更是得到了较大的发展，多次在国家级的戏剧赛事中取得良好的成绩。

2002 年，梨园戏作为中国“口头和非物质文化遗产”的典型代表，被亚太文化中心列入传统民间表演艺术数据库。

距今已有 800 多年历史的梨园戏，是南戏研究无法绕过的高峰，亦是中国仅存的宋元南戏遗存剧种之一，这是一座无形的综合艺术信息库。它深厚的戏曲文化积淀，在华夏戏剧史上有着突出地位。

天下之大，你也许走过许多地方的路，遇到许多地方的人，听过许多首歌谣。倘若没有听过梨园戏，这三百六十五里路，不免有一路的抱憾。

“中国戏剧奖·梅花表演奖”二度得主曾静萍主演的梨园戏《御碑亭》。（陈起拓 摄）

Yubei Pavilion (*Wang Youdao Divorces His Wife in Suspicion*) performed in Liyuan Opera by the two-time winner of “China Theater Plum Blossom Award”, Zeng Jingping. (Photo by Chen Qituo)

After the founding of the People's Republic of China, to protect Liyuan Opera as a traditional cultural heritage, the country and the cultural circles joined efforts in the rescue, innovation and inheritance of traditional repertoire, music and singing and performing arts of Liyuan Opera, which enables it to be greatly developed and achieve good results in many national drama competitions.

In 2002, as a typical representative of China's "Oral and Intangible Cultural Heritage", Liyuan Opera was listed in the databank of Traditional/Folk Performing Arts in Asia and the Pacific by the Asia Pacific Cultural Center (APCC).

With a history of more than 800 years and a profound opera culture heritage, Liyuan Opera, one of the few surviving plays of the Song and Yuan dynasties, is an intangible comprehensive databank of arts as well as a worthy topic of the study of Southern Opera.

In this big world of ours, you may have travelled many places, met many people and heard many musics. And Liyuan Opera is a feast to the ear which you can't afford to miss.

梨园戏表演走上街头。（陈起拓 摄）
Liyuan Opera performed on the street. (Photo by Chen Qituo)

高甲戏：角分九色，丑行亦挑大梁

徜徉老泉州，茶要一盅一盅啜，戏要一出一出看，在这般经典林立的“戏窝子”，稍一疏忽，就可能“入宝山而空手回”。而戏曲的宝藏，有文就有武，高甲戏就是后者的典范。

高甲戏，旧称“戈甲戏”“九角戏”，是福建五大剧种之一，风格独特。它孕育于明末清初，早期称“宋江仔”“宋江戏”，道光年间形成了“合兴班”，清末始称“高甲戏”。光听这迭变的戏名，你就能感受到它最初携带的一种尚武气质。

原来，高甲戏源于古代闽南民间迎神赛会中的装扮故事表演。明末清初，闽南民间流行化装游行，尤以泉州为盛，每逢喜庆吉日或迎神赛会，便有人装扮成梁山好汉，配以南锣、南鼓和民间“红甲吹”“十音”之类的曲调，游行于村镇，间或在广场上排成“蝴蝶阵”“长蛇阵”，进行带有故事性的表演，深受村民喜爱。后来逐渐发展成由儿童组成的业余戏班，演出剧目仍为宋江故事，群众称之为“宋江仔”。之后出现了由成人组成的专业戏班，时称“宋江戏”。宋江仔的兴起是高甲戏的孕育期，此后其与竹马戏、四平戏融合，艺术上获得发展，才逐渐形成了高甲戏。

高甲戏表演。（陈英杰 摄）
A performance of Gaojia Opera. (Photo by Chen Yingjie)

Gaojia Opera

One of the best loved pastimes in Quanzhou is to enjoy various operas over cups and cups of tea. You can easily miss one since the operas the city offers are so varied and dazzling. Among them are the singing plays characterized by singing and acting and the martial ones characterized by acrobatics and martial art performances. Gaojia Opera is a typical example of the latter.

Gaojia Opera, also Gejia Opera or Jiujiao Opera, is one of the five major theatrical genres in Fujian Province. It grew out of Song Jiang Zai or Song Jiang Opera, a folk performance that emerged in the late Ming Dynasty and early Qing Dynasty, which was mostly martial art when actors played as Liangshan heroes, legendary figures in one of the Four Great Classic Chinese Novels, *Water Margin* (*All Men Are Brothers*, Song Jiang being the main character). And then it developed into Hexing Opera, an art form that combined literature and martial art in the middle of the Qing Dynasty, absorbed elements of various opera styles and turned into Gaojia Opera in the late Qing Dynasty. The series of name changes, however, suggest its nature as a martial art play.

In the late Ming and early Qing dynasties, cosplay parades were popular among the folks in Southern Fujian, especially in Quanzhou. During festivals or in sacrifice ceremonies like God Pageant, people would dress up as Liangshan heroes and parade in villages and towns to the tunes of southern gongs, southern drums and local stringed and wind instruments. And occasionally, they would form butterfly arrays and snake arrays and act out stories. They were very popular with the villagers and gradually developed into amateur troupes made up of children, still performing the story of Song Jiang, known to the public as Song Jiang Zai (Junior Song Jiang Troupe). Later on, professional troupes of adults emerged, which were then called "Song Jiang Opera". The formation of the Junior Song Jiang Troupe which was later integrated with Zhuma Opera from Zhangzhou and Siping Opera from Ningde set the stage for the development of Gaojia Opera.

事实上，高甲戏的演出剧目大致分为大气戏（宫廷戏和武戏）、绣房戏和丑旦戏三大类，其中以武戏、丑旦戏和公案戏居多，生旦戏较少。高甲戏的角色原来只有生、旦、丑，后来又先后增加了净、贴、外、末和北（净）、杂二色。高甲戏的音乐唱腔兼用南曲、傀儡调和民间小调，以南曲为主。其形成和发展过程中，不断吸收本地兄弟剧种以及徽戏、弋阳腔、京剧等外来剧种的剧目、表演、音乐来丰富自身，艺术上日渐成熟。

在发展过程中，高甲戏还细分出许多流派，如柯派高甲戏，它的表演艺术代表人为"闽南名丑"柯贤溪。柯派表演身段能精细地呈现出从十八岁少女直到七八十岁老妪的不同特点，形成各个年龄段妇女风韵姿态的不同表演程式。柯贤溪于1960年参加厦门高甲戏丑角会演，被公推为"丑王"。此后柯派高甲戏丑行表演艺术日臻完美，代有传人，在闽南的泉州、厦门、漳州等地，中国的台湾、香港、澳门等地区和菲律宾等国家均有流布。

念兹在兹，一种戏曲的活态流布与缱绻共情，造就了跨文化传播的无限可能。长沟月去流无声，一切都交给舞台。那排空而来的老腔调，正呼应着你的心理调频，构筑起历史的天空，慰藉不老的情怀。

"来去看搬大戏啰！"入夜的泉州乡野，呼朋唤友的闽南腔此起彼伏，不绝于耳。懂戏之人，才懂人生。

高甲戏演员陈娟娟是2011年"中国戏剧奖·梅花表演奖"得主。（陈英杰 摄）
Chen Juanjuan, a Gaojia Opera actress, winner of the 2011 "China Theater Plum Blossom Award". (Photo by Chen Yingjie)

Plays of Gaojia Opera can be roughly divided into three categories, namely *daqi* (court and martial art) opera, *xiufang* (love stories) opera and *choudan* (comic roles) opera. There were only male roles, female roles and clowns in the beginning and other roles were added over time. Nanyin Music, together with puppet tunes and folk music, is used in the performance of Gaojia Opera. In the course of its formation and development, Gaojia Opera has constantly absorbed the repertoire, performances and music of local operas and those of others elsewhere like Hui Opera from Anhui, Yiyang Opera from Jiangxi and Peking Opera to enrich itself and become a unique genre of opera in its own right.

In the process of its development, Gaojia Opera has been subdivided into many schools, such as the Ke School of Gaojia Opera, whose performing art is represented by Ke Xianxi, the "most famous clown in Southern Fujian". The performance of the Ke School is characterized by different postures and gestures of females of all ages, be it an 18-year-old girl or a woman in her 70s or 80s. In 1960, Ke Xianxi took part in the Xiamen Gaojia Opera Clown Show and was voted "King of Clowns". Since then, the art of performing the clown roles of the Ke School has been perfected gradually and handed down from generation to generation. It is widespread not only in cities in Southern Fujian, such as Quanzhou, Xiamen and Zhangzhou, but also in regions of China like Taiwan, Hong Kong, Macao and countries like the Philippines.

Music knows no boundaries. It travels across time and space, nations and territories, calling for a true listener. It unites all of us, the young and the old, musicians and audience alike.

"Time for Gaojia Opera!" At the countryside of Quanzhou you can often hear people grabbing their friends to enjoy an opera together at night. He who knows opera is the one who knows life.

高甲戏登上中央广播电视总台 2019 春节戏曲晚会舞台。（陈英杰 摄）
Gaojia Opera mounted the stage of the 2019 Spring Festival Opera Gala of CMG. (Photo by Chen Yingjie)

打城戏：融贯佛道法事，打通天堂地狱

有这样一种戏，明明是戏曲表演，却浑似僧道法事，上“打天堂城”，下“打地狱城”。

你看那功夫十分了得：戏台上，连垒七八张桌子，戴着面具的演员一个凌空就从上面翻下来。如果这还不算特别，请你定睛细看，他的双手、腋下、嘴里、颈部一共夹着 11 个鸡蛋，翻桌动作完成，鸡蛋完好无损，而他则站在小板凳上，满是威仪。其后，更有叠罗汉、吃火吐火、吃纸拉肠、甩须、甩发、蚌舞、黑白鬼舞、叉舞、旗舞等特技。一番前戏过后，才上演“开大笼”的绝活，大笼里装着表演各种特殊类型舞蹈节目的面具、道具、衣饰，表演者可随着剧情需要，生动地展现公鸡与蜈蚣、雌雄鬼、鹰与蛇、虎与狼等互相搏斗的场面。演到高潮时，他们还会挑战难度系数更高的表演，引得观众连连惊叫，但总能有惊无险。

这种兼具宗教神秘色彩和感官娱乐属性的剧种，被闽南人称为“打城戏”。

打城戏（又名法事戏、师公戏、和尚戏）是清中叶在泉州、晋江一带的僧道法事仪式基础上演变发展而来的宗教剧种。“打城”仪式通常是在和尚或道士打醮拜忏圆满的最后一天举行的。一百多年后，它才跳出纯宗教仪式的圈子，开始出现在民间丧仪、盂兰盆会和水陆大醮等民俗活动中。

打城戏表演。（中新图片 供图）
A performance of Dacheng Opera. (Courtesy of CNSphoto.com)

Dacheng Opera

It is an opera but it looks more like the Buddhist and Taoist memorial rituals, in which the scenes of heaven and purgatory appear alternately.

Look! The kung fu is quite remarkable. Piled up there on the stage are seven or eight tables and an actor wearing a mask turns a somersault and flips down. If you don't think this is impressive enough, then watch closer. Held in his hands and mouth, under his arms and neck are eleven eggs in total, and when he flips down from the top of the tables to a stool composedly, the eggs are all intact. After that, there are more stunts such as building human pyramids, swallowing and spitting fire or paper, shaking the beard or the hair, clamshell dance, black and white ghost dance, fork dance and flag dance. These are all playlets and there comes the real masterstroke with the opening of the big chest, which is filled with masks, props and costumes for various types of dances. Performers can act out the fighting scenes of roosters and centipedes, male and female ghosts, eagles and snakes, tigers and wolves and those of other animals as required by the plot. At the climax, they will venture even more difficult tasks which wow the audience and take their breath away with near misses.

This opera which is both religiously mysterious and entertaining is called Dacheng Opera in Southern Fujian.

Dacheng Opera, also Ritual Opera, Taoist Opera or Monk's Opera, is a religious opera that evolves from the early Buddhist and Taoist memorial rituals in the middle of the Qing Dynasty. It was customarily performed on the last day of the rituals. It took around a century before Dacheng Opera, as a pure religious ritual, found its way into folk activities such as funerals, the Ghost Festival on the 15th of the 7th lunar month and heaven worship.

据晋江市小兴源村（也称小坑园村）《兴源里长房三族谱序》记载，大约在清咸丰十年（1860），兴源里吴永燎、吴永吟兄弟出面组织师公戏演出。英国牛津大学教授龙彼得则在海外文献中发现相关记载："1883年两位荷兰人在厦门观摩过打城戏的前身师公戏，演出的是《刘全进瓜果》。" 至1885年，小兴源村的师公戏已具备相当规模，培养了一批技艺精湛的演员，形成了自己的保留剧目。后来，泉州及晋江青阳、石狮、南安洪濑等地也成立了法事戏、师公戏与和尚戏戏班。中华人民共和国成立后，政府把晋江道教的小兴源班和泉州佛教的小开元班合并，并以他们共同的打城仪式为这种表演形式命名——打城戏。

泉州吴天乙打城戏剧团曾于2003年携传统剧目《目连救母》赴伊朗参加国际戏剧节，荣获"金小丑"奖；2004年赴日本参加中日韩戏剧节，演员谢幕五次，观众还不退场；2007年赴印度参加国际戏剧节，荣获"潘查尔"大奖。

戏曰打城，实则点悟众生；地狱天堂，其实都在人间。从道坛走向社会，从乡间走向舞台，从闽南走向世界，从眼睛走向心灵——打城戏，唱念做打之间，唯有对释道的崇敬，对艺术的朝觐，对人间的厚爱。

打城戏《目连救母》在台北演出。（中新图片 供图）
A traditional play of Dachen Opera, Monk Mulian Rescues His Mother, was performed in Taipei. (Courtesy of CNSphoto.com)

The earliest record of the opera can probably be found in *Preface to the Genealogy of the Three Clans of the Eldest Branch of Xingyuanli* in Xiaoxingyuan Village (also Xiaokengyuan Village) in Jinjiang City, when the two brothers Wu Yongliao and Wu Yongyin provided Shigong Opera (Taoist Opera), the antecedent of Dacheng Opera in around 1860. While Piet van der Loon, a professor at Oxford University in the UK, found a relevant record in overseas literature: "In 1883 two Dutchmen were in Xiamen to observe a Shigong Opera, the predecessor of Dacheng Opera, titled *Liu Quan Worshiped God with Fruits*." By 1885, Shigong Opera in Xiaoxingyuan Village had been well-developed with its own group of skilled performers and stock repertoire. Later, troupes of Ritual Opera, Taoist Opera and Monk's Opera were established in places like Quanzhou, Qingyang, Shishi and Honglai. After the founding of the People's Republic of China in 1949, the government merged the Taoist troupe, Xiaoxingyuan Troupe in Jinjiang with the Buddhist troupe, Xiaokaiyuan Troupe in Quanzhou and named this performance Dacheng Opera after their common ritual ceremony.

In 2003, Quanzhou Wu Tianyi Centre for Dacheng Opera Heritage of Fujian went to Iran to participate in the international theater festival with the traditional play *Monk Mulian Rescues His Mother* and won the "Golden Clown" award. Then, in 2004, it went to Japan to participate in the BeSeTo Theater Festival, during which the actors made five curtain calls, but the audience did not leave. In 2007, it went to India to participate in the international theater festival and won the "Panchal" award.

More than a ritual opera, Dacheng Opera is an enlightenment for all beings. Heaven and purgatory are actually all on earth. From a Taoist ritual to a folk activity, from the countryside to the stage, from Southern Fujian to the world, from eyes to soul, Dacheng Opera is but the reverence for Buddhism and Taoism, the tribute to art and the love for the world.

传统美术：
触手成春，徜徉温陵不忍归

Traditional Folk Crafts

泉州花灯：天下上元，灯烛之盛，无逾闽中

Quanzhou Lanterns

惠安石雕：北有曲阳，南有惠安

Hui' an Stone Carvings

泉州（李尧宝）刻纸：刀尖下的花花世界

Quanzhou (Li Yaobao) Paper-Carvings

泉州（江加走）木偶头雕刻：承唐宋雕技，臻神人化境

Quanzhou (Jiang Jiazou) Puppet Heads

永春纸织画：是真非真画非画，经纬既见分纵横

Yongchun Paper-Woven Pictures

安溪竹藤编：经纬有度，深山竹藤编万物

Anxi Bamboo and Rattan Weavings

泉州木雕：泉郡名匠，善雕浮屠花卉

Quanzhou Wood Carvings

泉州花灯：
天下上元，灯烛之盛，无逾闽中

在明代遗老兼大才子张岱那本笔记体回忆录《陶庵梦记》中，一个城市的花灯往事赫然浮出水面：杭州抚台委托泉州府尹和南安（泉州下辖县）知县雇人精制花灯，并盛赞泉州花灯“穷工极巧，造灯十架，凡两年成”“十年不得坏”。足见当时泉州花灯质量之上乘、工艺之精湛，已闻名遐迩。

只是张岱也许不知道，泉州花灯制作早在唐代就已有不小规模，至宋、元两代已蔚然成风。宋代梁克家《三山志》载：“泉州花灯品种色色俱全，莲花灯、百花灯、琉璃灯……”可见当时泉州花灯品种之丰富。明代谢肇淛所著《五杂俎》则写道：“天下上元，灯烛之盛，无逾闽中。”这里所说的“闽中”即泉州，可以想见当时泉州元宵夜的花灯盛况。

花灯照亮泉州元宵节。（陈英杰 摄）
Thousands of lanterns lit up the whole city of Quanzhou during the Lantern Festival. (Photo by Chen Yingjie)

Quanzhou Lanterns

The superior quality, the exquisite workmanship and the good name of Quanzhou Lanterns are well documented in the collection of prose, *Dream Reminiscence of Tao'an*, written by the late Ming eminent scholar, Zhang Dai (1597—1689). As is written, the then military governor of Hangzhou entrusted the prefectural magistrate of Quanzhou and the prefect of Nan'an (a county under Quanzhou) to hire craftsmen to tailor make lanterns for him. It took them two years to make ten lanterns which were extremely beautiful and delicate and could last for ten years.

Zhang, however, might not be aware of the fact that the craftsmanship of lantern-making in Quanzhou had already reached a considerable level as early as in the Tang Dynasty and became very popular in the Song and Yuan dynasties. There was an account of the great variety of Quanzhou Lanterns in *Records of the Three Mountains*, a local gazetteer of Fujian Province written during the Southern Song period (1127—1279) by Chen Fuliang and later revised by Liang Kejia. Whereas the busy and festive atmosphere of the Lantern Festival in Quanzhou was depicted by the Ming Dynasty writer Xie Zhaozhe in his reading notes, *The Five Assorted Offerings*.

泉州花灯传习所林伟忠正在制作五福花灯。（陈小阳 摄）
Lin Weizhong is making blessing lanterns at Quanzhou Lantern Workshop. (Photo by Chen Xiaoyang)

泉州花灯从制作工艺来说主要分为彩扎灯、刻纸灯、针刺无骨灯三大类。其中后两者为泉州花灯的突出代表，是全国罕见的花灯品种。刻纸料丝灯是用几十乃至几百个几何图形的纸板合并成立体灯体，纸板上均刻有各种各样镂空的精美图案，并镶上料丝，精美绝伦，且能靠着薄壳结构的力学原理均匀地支撑整个灯体，无须绑扎灯骨架。针刺无骨灯也是用许许多多立体几何图形的纸板合成灯体，但此类纸板的图案并非用刀刻成，而是以针尖刺扎，光源从针孔中透出，显得灯体晶莹剔透。这两者采用的制作工艺在全国绝无仅有，独树一帜。因工艺之特殊，泉州花灯灯会曾先后登陆中国台湾地区及菲律宾、新加坡、加拿大、美国等国家，广受欢迎。一些华人较多的国家每年都有华侨商家订制泉州花灯，以庆祝元宵节或中秋节。

作为一种手艺性极强的行业，泉州花灯制作的传承可谓不易，如今硕果仅存的手艺人基本来自清同治年间开业的老招牌“金传胪”和始自清末民初的李尧宝家族、陈昌士家族等。特别值得一提的是，李尧宝大师首创了刻纸料丝花灯，把独特的刻纸技艺和图案应用到花灯的造型制作中，使泉州花灯的制作工艺、视觉效果和技术含量均产生了重大飞跃。1959 年，李尧宝花灯被送往北京展出，向国庆十周年献礼，国家主席刘少奇看了很感兴趣，并在花灯前与李尧宝合影留念。其后李氏作品更是成了艺术瑰宝，被作为国家礼品馈赠外宾，跨越五洲四海，架设友谊桥梁。

“灯火里的中国，青春婀娜；灯火里的中国，胸怀辽阔。”

一个在月下追光的时代，必然会获得属于它的高光时刻；一个向往光明的族群，前景不言自明。

泉州无骨花灯制作。（陈英杰 摄）
The making of Quanzhou frameless lanterns. (Photo by Chen Yingjie)

There are three major types of Quanzou Lanterns: the bamboo and silk lantern, the paper-carving lantern and the stitch-pierced frameless lantern, the latter two of which are more famous for their rarity. For a paper-carving silk lantern, there is a three-dimensional body made up of dozens or even hundreds of cardboards which are engraved with a variety of exquisite hollowed-out patterns and inlaid with filaments. The mechanic principle helps the thin-shelled structure to support the whole lamp without a bamboo framework. For a stitch-pierced frameless lantern, there is also a three-dimensional body made up of many cardboards with geometric shapes, only that these cardboards are not carved but pierced with the tip of a needle and the light comes out of the pinholes, making the whole lantern crystal like. The craftsmanship for making these two types of lanterns is so unique that it makes Quanzhou lantern shows well received in regions like Taiwan and countries like the Philippines, Singapore, Canada and the US. Every year, overseas Chinese businesses in countries with a large ethnic Chinese population order a lot of Quanzhou Lanterns for the celebration of the Lantern Festival and Mid-Autumn Festival.

As a highly artisanal profession, to impart and inherit the techniques of making Quanzhou Lanterns is very difficult, and the only surviving craftsmen today mainly come from those time-honoured shops such as Jinchuanlu of the late Qing Dynasty and Li Yaobao and Chen Changtu families of the late Qing and early Republican period. It is worth mentioning that Master Li Yaobao pioneered the paper-carving silk lanterns and applied the unique carving skills and patterns to the modeling of lanterns, which made a great leap in the making, visual effect and craftsmanship of Quanzhou Lanterns. In 1959, one of Li's works was sent to Beijing for exhibition as a tribute for the 10th anniversary of the National Day, the then President of China, Liu Shaoqi, was very much impressed and took a photo with Li in front of the lantern. Since then, Li's works, as the treasure of traditional Chinese arts, have been presented to foreign guests as national gifts.

As is sung, "China in the light is young and graceful; China in the light is open-minded and generous."

This is a time of peace and prosperity and this is the time of the great rejuvenation of the Chinese nation. Many traditional arts like Quanzhou Lanterns have sprung back to life and like the lanterns, they will definitely light our way of realizing the Chinese Dream.

惠安石雕：北有曲阳，南有惠安

“人猿相揖别。只几个石头磨过，小儿时节。”新旧石器时代的划分，野蛮向文明进化的分野，女娲补天的传说，四大名著的演绎……石头始终是文明的见证者。

泉州惠安，一个在史前已有人类生存的地方，随着晋唐衣冠南渡、中原文化传入，形成了丰富的手工业文明。北宋太平兴国六年（981）惠安置县，舟楫汇通海外诸夷；明清两代，战略地位凸显，跻身闽南重镇。而在其崇武半岛一带，因土地贫瘠，百姓因地制宜，一则讨海为生，二则利用当地石蛋地形遍地裸露的岩石发展石雕工艺，使其渐渐发展壮大，一发而不可收。

惠安石雕早期用于宗教场合，具有浓厚的宗教色彩，这主要体现在它对宫观寺庙中塔、亭、柱、栏以及神佛造像出神入化的雕刻上。惠安石雕在每个不同的历史时期都留有蕴含特定历史信息的精品，如宋代的桥、塔、寺，明清的蟠龙石柱、石狮子及其他古建筑、古民居。无论是1,600多年前晋代开闽始祖林禄墓前的石雕，还是唐末五代时期闽王王审知兄长王潮墓前巧夺天工的艺术神品，无一不显示出当地工匠先贤的精湛技艺。宋元时期，惠安石雕工艺更是大放异彩，“海内第一桥”洛阳桥的兴建，惠安崇武古城的崛起，无不留下其杰作。

惠安崇武石雕工艺博览园里的罗汉林。（视觉中国 供图）
Arhat statues in China Stone Carving Craft Expo Park in Chongwu Ancient Town of Hui'an County. (Courtesy of VCG.COM)

Hui'an Stone Carvings

It seems that stones have always been part of our civilization. The use of stones realizes the evolution of apes into human beings. Nyu Wa, the goddess of order who created humans in Chinese mythology, mended the huge hole in the sky with colored stones. And *The Story of the Stone*, also known by the title of *The Dream of the Red Chamber*, is one of the Four Classic Novels in Chinese literature.

Hui'an County in Quanzhou, a place where human being habitation dates back to prehistoric times, boasts all kinds of craftsmanship which was developed with the southward migrations of the imperial clans from the Central Plains during the West Jin and Tang dynasties (266—907). When Hui'an became a county in 981, it had boats sailing to various overseas countries. During the Ming and Qing dynasties, the county's strategic position was highlighted and it became one of the most important counties in Southern Fujian. In Chongwu Peninsula where the county lies, the land was so barren that people had to struggle for a living. Some made a living by fishing while others made use of its pebbly landform to develop the stone carving industry which grew gradually till it led the pack.

Hui'an Stone Carvings, in the early phrase, were rich in religious connotation, for they appeared mainly in religious sites and the super craftsmanship was best exemplified in the carvings of statutes of gods and Buddhas as well as the pagodas, pavilions, columns and railings in different palaces and temples. Different historical periods have gifted us with different masterpieces of Hui'an Stone Carvings, such as the bridges, pagodas and temples from the Song Dynasty, the dragon-wrapped columns and stone lions from the Ming and Qing dynasties and the ancient buildings and folk houses. The tomb stones of Lin Lu, founder of Fujian in the Jin Dynasty more than 1,600 years ago and those of Wang Chao, the elder brother of Wang Shenzhi, the vassal king of the Min Kingdom on the southeast coastal province of Fujian in China during the Five Dynasties and Ten Kingdoms period both showcase the super craftsmanship of Hui'an artisans. Even more brilliant Hui'an Carvings appeared in the building of "the No. 1 Stone Bridge", Luoyang Bridge, in Quanzhou and Chongwu Ancient Town in Hui'an, both of which were built during the Song and Yuan dynasties.

大开大合的神斧并未阻碍其追逐精耕细作的艺术脚步，至明末清初，惠安石雕风格开始从粗犷流畅转向精雕细琢，终于以具“杏花春雨江南”般婉约精细的独特艺术风格成为南派石雕艺术的典型代表，独擎中国石雕艺术的半壁江山。

花开神州，香飘四海。明万历年间，惠安石雕的身影就已出现在菲律宾。清代中期，惠安石雕开始在中国台湾地区广受追捧，成为闽台交往的重要载体。建筑无声，却是历史与文化最好的言说者。惠安石雕因其强烈的民族审美属性、鲜明的时代性、丰富的表达性及艺术的独创性，成为活跃在每一个时代建筑舞台中央的挑大梁者。

如今，在东南亚一带，惠安石雕的技法依然泽被深远；而从国家到地方的重大建筑工程中，惠安石雕也不遑多让。“北有曲阳，南有惠安”已被中国石雕界广泛认可，而南派石雕的辉煌还在延续，十几万惠安石雕匠人遍布全国二十多个省（自治区、直辖市），就是一个生动的数据证明。

时间说明一切，一种技艺为石头的隐喻作出最佳注脚。忆往昔，它曾是逗落秋雨的石破天，也曾是造富于民的石中玉；望未来，它更是扬帆海丝的压舱宝，赓续泉州文明的奠基石。

中国共产党历史展览馆广场的大型惠安石雕《追梦》。（李文敬 摄）

The large-scale Hui'an stone sculpture *Chasing Dreams* in the square of Museum of the Communist Party of China. (Photo by Li Wenjing)

Hui'an people never stop surpassing themselves and perfecting their skills. By the late Ming and early Qing period, stone carvings of Hui'an had changed from rough and simple to elegant and exquisite, a unique style which made it a typical representative of the southern school of stone carvings.

As early as in the Wanli period (1573—1628) of the Ming Dynasty, Hui'an Stone Carvings were exported to the Philippines. And in the middle of the Qing Dynasty, they were so widely sought after in Taiwan that they helped enhance the interaction and exchanges between Taiwan and Southern Fujian. With unique aesthetic and historic value, masterpieces of Hui'an Stone Carvings from different eras became time stamps and have been the best storytellers of our history and culture.

Influence of Hui'an Stone Carvings can be found in the buildings in some of the Southeast Asian countries. In our major national and local construction projects, stone carvings from Hui'an are also indispensable. In terms of stone carvings, Quyang stone carvings are the best representative of the northern school, whereas Hui'an, that of the southern school. The number of one hundred thousand or more artisans from Hui'an working nationwide is an endorsement of its high recognition.

A pioneer in its own trade, the super craftsmanship of Hui'an Stone Carvings gives life to stones and earns a living for people. They had, did and will play their part in the maritime culture.

惠安女工匠正在制作民用石雕。（陈英杰 摄）
Women craftsmen in Hui'an are making stone carvings for domestic use. (Photo by Chen Yingjie)

以石为纸、雕琢岁月的惠安石雕。（汪洪波 摄）
Hui'an Stone Carvings, magic on stones. (Photo by Wang Hongbo)

泉州（李尧宝）刻纸：刀尖下的花花世界

一项非遗代表作，竟是从垃圾堆里获得灵感，继而惊艳世界，这种事你闻所未闻，却真实地发生在泉州。

20 世纪 50 年代初，一位泉州老艺人在晋江一户富家祠堂承揽油漆画工程时，偶然拾得半个废弃的料丝灯球。饶有兴致地把玩之余，他猛地醍醐灌顶，神谕般的灵感掠过心头，令他无数次碰壁的艺术天花板，在此刻砉然而破。

此人，就是日后被誉为“中国刻纸艺术大师”的李尧宝。我们不禁要问，小小刻纸，究竟有何神奇？一切还得从泉州特殊的传统说起。泉州灯彩刻纸制作承袭唐宋技法，一向以富丽堂皇而著称。但彼时，八闽大地传统的刻纸仅限于供应春节及喜庆场合的“红笺”“福符”。而无骨料丝花灯始于明朝，由云南人以紫石英、玛瑙为原料捣料混炼，抽丝缠成球状灯具，再于其上施以绘画，后流传到江苏丹阳，清代初期又流传入京，至清末由没落的八旗子弟将手艺带至福建，民国时期因战乱一度失传。

就在人们都以为神技不可再现之时，李尧宝却从垃圾堆里的料丝灯球中找到了突破路径。他悉心研究此球，创造性地结合家传的刻纸及油漆画技艺，以无骨架、手工镂刻纸板、手工三层叠彩绘、通体镶嵌料丝四大要素作为作品灵魂，由此创作出由 165 个等边三角形构成的球状无骨刻纸料丝花灯——多角灯，继而成为刻纸料丝花灯的继承人与创新者。

泉州（李尧宝）刻纸传承人、李尧宝外孙女黄丽凤（左）和母亲在一起。（陈英杰 摄）
Huang Lifeng (left), granddaughter of Master Li Yaobao as well as the inheritor of Quanzhou (Li Yaobao) Paper-Carvings, is with her mother. (Photo by Chen Yingjie)

Quanzhou (Li Yaobao) Paper-Carvings

It must be something unheard of that an item that enters the representative list of intangible cultural heritage and amazes the world should have been inspired by a junk. Yet it really happened in Quanzhou.

In the early 1950s, an old artisan was contracted to paint the ancestral hall of a wealthy family in Jinjiang when he happened to pick up a half-discarded glass-silk lamp bulb. While he was turning it over and over with great interest, an idea struck him.

The artisan was Li Yaobao, who was later hailed as "Master of Chinese Paper-Carvings". One cannot help but wonder what is so magical about his little piece of paper-carvings? It all starts with the special tradition of lantern making in Quanzhou. Carved cardboard lanterns of Quanzhou has always been known for their grandeur and splendour and was inherited from the Tang and Song dynasties, when the traditional paper-carvings in Fujian were limited to the supply of "red paper" and "lucky charms" for Chinese New Year and festive occasions. The frameless glass-silk lanterns appeared during the Ming Dynasty, when craftsmen in Yunnan mixed amethyst and agate to extract glass-silk which they wrapped into ball-shaped lamps and lanterns and then painted on them. It was later spread to Danyang, Jiangsu, then introduced to Beijing in the early Qing Dynasty and in the late Qing Dynasty, brought to Fujian by the declining Eight-Banner descendants, but was lost because of war during the Republican period.

When people were regretting the loss, Li, inspired by the glass-silk lamp bulb, further developed it by applying his family paper-carving and painting skills to the making of multi-angle glass-silk lanterns. The new frameless lantern had 165 equilateral triangles which were made of hand-carved cardboards with a triple-layered hand painting. Li himself became an inheritor and innovator of paper-carving silk lanterns.

此后，勇攀艺术高峰的泉州人李尧宝又不断创作出形态、规格各不相同的料丝花灯品种。李尧宝刻纸作品内容丰富，题材广泛，有人们喜闻乐见的飞禽走兽、人物、花卉；有象征吉祥的博古、交枝曲己、瓜果鱼虫等。其作品构图奔放自如，布局紧凑，疏密得当，一气呵成，层次分明，繁而不乱。其刻纸图案既富有国画白描的笔姿，又有刀刻挺拔的风韵。其画面黑白对比强烈，虚实阴阳兼用，手法细腻，以对称、放射、连续、对角等形式体现着优美、工整、清新、鲜明的独特艺术风格，让人久望而不烦。其刻纸技艺集中呈现于龙凤、吉庆、博古、花鸟、交枝、人物六大类别，其中以博古图案、交枝曲己图案最具闽南地方特色，形象造型古朴典雅，立意深远，博古知今。其刻工纤毫毕露，刚柔并济，技法巧妙。其成品造型新奇独特，优雅秀丽，栩栩如生。

高超的技艺令李尧宝誉满中外。1960 年 11 月 8 日，董必武来泉州工艺厂参观李尧宝作品时题字：“丰富多彩，意匠生新，能见其大，能传其神。”

以一人之力，独擎南方剪纸流派大旗，让神技重现于世，真正的工匠精神，在于此，也在泉州。

泉州（李尧宝）刻纸创作现场。（陈起拓 摄）
The scene of creating Quanzhou (Li Yaobao) Paper-Carvings. (Photo by Chen Qituo)

Since then, Li Yaobao, a native Quanzhou artist, never stopped his pursuit of silk lanterns with different shapes and specifications. Li's paper carvings, integrated with traditional Chinese line drawings, cover a wide range of themes, including birds and animals, figures and flowers as well as symbols of good fortune, such as ancient artifacts, cross branches, fruits, fish and insects. His paper carvings fall into six major categories: the dragon and phoenix, celebrations, ancient artifacts, birds and flowers, cross branches and figures, among which the line-based and block-based patterns of artifacts and cross branches with simple and elegant designs and profound connotations are of Southern Fujian characteristic. Exquisite, neat, fresh and unique, Li's paper carvings are impressive. Adopting patterns ranging from symmetrical, radial, continuous to diagonal ones and forming a sharp contrast between black and white, his works are free and unrestrained in composition, novel, elegant and lifelike in design, powerful and smooth in carving.

The super craftsmanship brought Li Yaobao popular fame. On November 8, 1960, when Dong Biwu, the then vice president of China, visited Quanzhou Craft Factory and appreciated Li's works, he wrote down his comments, "The great variety of works has great originality and vividly reflects the profound Chinese culture."

Thanks to Li's tireless pursuit of art, the lost techniques were brought back to life and the southern school of paper cuttings was established. And this best explains what real craftsmanship is.

泉州（江加走）木偶头雕刻：承唐宋雕技，臻神人化境

“刀未出手前，谁也想象不到它的速度和力量。大家只知道一件事——刀一定在它应该在的地方。”这是武侠小说家古龙描绘小李飞刀的师父“边城浪子”叶开的名句。

若是拿这句话形容一代大师江加走的神技，也毫无违和感。只不过，江加走的刀，只雕木偶。

对于傀儡戏而言，傀儡头是木偶造型的关键之处，谁能掌握这个核心技术，谁就拥有了笑傲偶坛的底气。泉州雕技有得天独厚的优势，本土傀儡头造型完美保留了雍容丰腴、神韵含蓄的艺术风格。

江加走的大师之路似乎有些命中注定。江加走与哥哥江凹司幼时都读过几年私塾，后因家贫辍学。江加走 11 岁开始学艺，15 岁已学会很多雕刻手艺，17 岁因父亲眼力衰退不能工作，他就开始继承父业。18 岁时，父亲病逝，他与哥哥共同挑起生活的担子。江加走子承父业，学做木偶头坯的雕刻，哥哥做木偶头粉彩。兄弟俩孜孜不倦，技艺上不断精进，在木偶头的制作上精准分工合作。哥哥去世后，江加走把木偶头像的粉彩工作也担当起来，全面继承了父业。

凭借父亲传授给他的 50 多种木偶头像和一种叫“平髻”的梳头方式，江加走悉心钻研。少年时代，他就对泉州木偶雕刻老字号周冕号艺人黄良司、黄才司所创作的木偶头像特别感兴趣，经常到作坊研磨学习其造型和技艺，吸取前辈和同辈艺人的宝贵经验。历经多年打磨，依靠惊人的天赋和创作力，他继承发展和创作了 285 种不同性格的木偶头像，新编梳十余种不同式样的头髻和发辫，雕刻和粉彩的木偶头像达万余件之多，最终成为木偶制作领域的一代大师。

江加走木偶头雕刻作品。（王柏峰 摄）
Puppet heads carved by Jiang Jiazou. (Photo by Wang Baifeng)

Quanzhou (Jiang Jiazou) Puppet Heads

"When the knife is still at hand, no one knows how powerful and fast it can be. All we know is that the knife belongs where it should be." This is quoted from the description of a master of knives in one of the martial arts novels by Gu Long.

It is the right depiction of the techniques of Master Jiang Jiazou as well. Only that his knife is used in the carving of puppet heads.

Puppet heads are the essential parts of puppet shows and whoever makes the best puppet heads takes the lead in the trade. The unique carving techniques of Quanzhou craftsmen make their puppet heads full and round, graceful and poised.

Jiang Jiazou's becoming a master carver is probably all written in the stars. He and his elder brother, Jiang Aosi attended a few years' old-style private school when young and dropped out of school later due to poverty. He became an apprentice of carving when he's eleven and he was quite a carver when he's fifteen. At the age of 17, he started to learn puppet head carving when his father was forced to retired due to failing eyesight. One year later, his father passed away and he and his brother had to make their own living by taking up their father's puppet head carving business, Jiang Jiazou doing the carving while his brother the painting. The two brothers shared out the work and cooperated with each other. They worked so hard to perfect their craftsmanship that they soon made great progress. However, after his brother's death, Jiang Jiazou had to take on both the carving and painting of puppet heads on his own.

Jiang Jiazou soaked himself in the carving of more than fifty different puppet heads with flat buns that his father taught him. In his boyhood, he was particularly interested in the modeling and crafts of mater carvers like Huang Liangsi and Huang Caisi from the time-honored puppet carving store called Zhou Mian Hao, so he went to their workshop to learn from them and other fellow carvers. With his perseverance as well as his talent and creativity, he bettered and created 285 different puppet heads with more than ten hair styles. Carving and painting ten thousand or more puppet heads, he finally became a master of puppet head carvings himself.

1920 年对于江加走来说意义非凡。他成功制作了《封神演义》全套木偶头像，声名大振。当时，凡闽南木偶戏师傅演新戏需创作新木偶头像，都会去找他计议。又因周冕号的老艺人先后染疫亡故，江加走就承揽了从泉州、漳州、厦门、福州到南洋各地的提线、掌中木偶头的雕刻和粉彩业务。他创作的大量木偶头精品除了供闽南泉、漳、厦地区木偶戏演出使用，还出现在世界各地的木偶戏演出中。20 世纪 50 年代，随着泉州木偶戏剧团到上海、苏州及北京等地演出，后来又到罗马尼亚参加国际木偶节，江加走以木偶头像制作成就闻名海内外，被国际友人誉为“木偶之父”。

一把刻刀，无所不在，无所不至。小小木偶，五形三骨之间，美、丑、忠、奸，往往活灵活现；雅、俗、贤、愚，总能纤毫毕现。人世间的喜怒哀乐，都在这具体而微的艺术造型里。大师的触手成春，能把“死”木头变成“活”木偶，给予一个舞台鲜活的灵魂。

2008 年 CCTV《寻宝》栏目评选出的泉州“民间国宝”——江加走掌中木偶。（王柏峰 摄）
In 2008, glove puppets made by Jiang Jiazou were selected as "Folk National Treasures" of Quanzhou by CCTV's hit show, *Treasure Hunting*. (Photo by Wang Baifeng)

The year 1920 was of great significance for Jiang Jiazou. He became famous as he made it to carve a set of puppet heads for the figures in the Ming Dynasty historical romance, *The Investiture of the Gods*, ordered by a puppet troupe. After that, whenever puppeteers in Southern Fujian needed new puppet heads for their new shows, they would turn to him. And after master carvers of Zhou Mian Hao died of epidemic diseases, he became the sole contractor of puppet heads for both marionette and glove puppet shows in Quanzhou, Zhangzou, Xiamen, Fuzhou and some Southeast Asian countries. Masterpieces of his not only showed up in performances of puppet troupes in cities of Southern Fujian, but also toured around the world with these troupes. In the 1950s, with Quanzhou Marionette Troupe, they appeared in stages of Shanghai, Suzhou and Beijing and later attended the Romanian International Puppet Festival which made Jiang's puppet heads widely known and thus won him the title "Father of Puppets".

The carving of the face, especially the two eyes, one mouth, two nostrils, eyebrows, cheekbones and chin, is particularly important in the overall shape of a puppet. Puppets made by Jiang Jiazou never failed to portray the diverse nuances of different figures, be they beautiful, ugly, loyal or wicked; elegant, vulgar, talented or silly. It took the magic hands of a master to turn pieces of lifeless wood into lively characters on the stage.

江派木偶头雕刻第四代传承人黄雪玲作品——白素贞。（黄雪玲 供图）

Bai Suzhen, a Chinese mythological figure carved by Huang Xueling, the fourth generation inheritor of the Jiang School Puppet Heads Carvings. (Courtesy of Huang Xueling)

永春纸织画：
是真非真画非画，经纬既见分纵横

永春，因“众水会于桃溪一源”，古称桃源。相传隋唐年间，春天的桃溪两岸桃花盛开，薄雾如轻纱隐隐笼罩，这种雾中观花的独特体验激发了当时艺人的创作灵感，纸织画便应运而生。唐人郑维曾赋诗称颂纸织画：“何物离披最可人，纸间经纬别有因；阿谁巧作维摩手，就里挥毫称绝伦。”宋元时永春纸织画远销南洋各埠，成为富贵人家的柜中珍品。明人田艺蘅所撰《留青日札》中记载：“嘉靖间，没严嵩家物，已有纸织字画。”清代杨复吉《梦兰琐笔》中则记载：“闽中永春州织画，以罗纹笺剪为片，五色相间，经纬成纹，凡山水、人物、花鸟皆具。”故宫博物院至今仍珍藏着清代乾隆年间的纸织画《清高宗御制诗十二扇屏风》。

永春纸织画与杭州丝织画、苏州缂丝画、四川竹帘画并称中国的“四大家织”。据《永春州志》卷十一记载：“织画此为永春特产。其法以佳纸作字或画，乃剪为长条细缕而以纯白之条缕经纬之，然后加以彩色。与古所谓罨画及香笔记挈画相类。”

永春纸织画。（永春县文旅局 供图）
A piece of Yongchun Paper-Woven Picture. (Courtesy of Tourism Bureau of Yongchun County, Quanzhou City)

Yongchun Paper-Woven Pictures

Yongchun County was known as Taoyuan (peach source) in ancient times because many waters met at Taoyuan Stream here. Legend has it that during the Sui and Tang dynasties (581—907), every spring when peach trees were in full bloom on both sides of Taoyuan Stream, they looked hazy but beautiful when enveloped in mists. Inspired by the unique scene, local artists created the paper-woven pictures. The poet, Zheng Wei of the Tang Dynasty, once wrote a poem in praise of the strange beauty and originality of the paper-woven pictures. During the Song and Yuan dynasties, Yongchun Paper-Woven Pictures were sold to some Southeast Asian countries, including the Malay Archipelago, the Malay Peninsula and Indonesia, where they were treasured up by the rich. The Ming Dynasty writer, Tian Yiheng, surmised in his book about social customs and stories of the art circle in the Ming Dynasty that as Yongchun Paper-Woven Pictures and calligraphy were among the treasures found in the house of Yan Song, a corrupt official, the picture must have been popular since the Ming Dynasty. Yang Fuji, the bibliophile and writer of the Qing Dynasty, described in his ghost novel the materials, skills and major themes of Yongchun Paper-Woven Pictures. Kept in the National Palace Museum today are the twelve screens of paper-woven pictures dated from the Qing Dynasty, inside which contain the poems composed by Emperor Qianlong.

Yongchun Paper-Woven Pictures, along with Hangzhou Silk Brocade Paintings, Suzhou Kesi Tapestries and Sichuan Painted Bamboo Curtains, are known as the "Four Best Weaving Products of China". According to *Yongchun Local Gazetteer*, the paper woven picture is a specialty of Yongchun and the skills of making it are similar to those of the mixed color painting in the old days: First write or paint on a fine paper before cutting it into long strips, weave in the pure white ones and then color it.

永春纸织画的制作过程十分精细，有画、裁、织、裱褙等工序。制作时先在一张宣纸上绘好图画，再用一种特制的小刀按一定规格仔细地裁成一条条纤细的纸条，宽度在 2 到 3 毫米之间，头尾不断，保持一致，此为经线；再取洁白宣纸，裁成规格和经线一样的纸条，此为纬线；然后用特制的纸织机，双梭交穿，轻轻细织；最后根据画面需要，补上各种颜色。成品纸痕交织，经纬分明，画面朦胧，极富立体感。

近代纸织画著名艺人黄永源在其《纸织画旨趣》中总结了纸织画的特色“二性”，即色彩淡雅性和朦胧隐约性。纸织画的色彩本是浓艳的，而经过裁和织，再以一条条白色纬线盖上去，色彩被掩盖了一半，十分颜色只能看到四分，于是就产生了色彩的淡雅性，大大提高了纸织画成品的艺术格调。朦胧隐约性就是似有似无的画面效果，纸织画“近视几不类物象，远视则景物粲然”，与宋代著名画家米芾的“米点山水”有着异曲同工之妙。此外，纸织画还具有浅浮雕般的立体感。

纸织画所选择的题材很广泛，山水花鸟、飞禽走兽、历史人物、神话故事、民间传说应有尽有。“莫把丹青等闲看，无声诗里颂千秋”，近精微致广大的纸织画，恰似一首无声的诗歌，在岁月的流淌中，低诉着一个时代的大写风流。

墨笔丹青，如行云流水绕素笺，展瀚海崇山依旧颜，怎一个“好”字了得。

永春纸织画传承人方碧双正在创作。（刘宝生 摄）
Fang Bishuang, the inheritor of Yongchun Paper-Woven Pictures, is creating. (Photo by Liu Baosheng)

To make a Yongchun paper-woven picture involves complicated procedures, including drawing and painting, cutting, weaving and mounting. First, draw a picture on a piece of rice paper and use a special knife to cut it into thin paper strips of two to three millimeters in width without separating from the two ends and use them as the warp. Then take another piece of white rice paper, cut it into the same size to serve as the weft. After that, use a special paper loom to weave carefully. Finally, various colors are added according to the needs of the picture. The interwoven strips give the picture a sense of haziness and make it more lively.

Huang Yongyuan, a famous artist of modern paper-woven pictures, summed up the two characteristics of it in his book, *Ins and Outs of Paper-Woven Pictures*, namely, the lightness of the color and the haziness of the image. The color of the paper-woven picture is otherwise rich, but as it is cut and woven and covered with the white weft, the hue is reduced by half, thus producing the elegance of the color, which greatly improves the artistic beauty of the finished paper-woven picture. The picture half covered now is vague when looked closer and clear when looked from a distance. It reminds the audience of how it feels to look at the landscape painting created with various shades of ink dots called "Mi-Family Dots" by Mi Pei and his son, Mi Youren, two famous painters of the Song Dynasty. Only that the paper-woven picture looks like a bas-relief.

Yongchun Paper-Woven Pictures cover a wide range of subjects, including landscape, flowers, birds, animals, historical figures, myths and folklore. They are the transcribers of our time and history as well as an ode to Chinese traditional craftsmanship.

A small picture presents to us the whole world and culture.

周氏纸织画作品《宋元中国 海丝泉州》百米长卷创作现场。（视觉中国 供图）

Quanzhou: A Maritime Emporium in Song-Yuan China, a hundred-meter paper-woven picture, is being created by the Zhou Family. (Courtesy of VCG.COM)

安溪竹藤编：经纬有度，深山竹藤编万物

竹之空心耿介，顶天立地，无异于君子象征，历代文人总是不吝赞颂。全国产竹之地甚多，但一个县有15万人以竹编为业，且被授予“中国藤铁工艺之都”“世界手工艺理事会手工艺城市——藤铁工艺之都”称号的，恐怕只有安溪。

安溪，一个以铁观音闻名于世的泉州西部县城，早在唐末，已盛行竹藤编织。《五代初建安溪县记》记载：“……坐肆列邸，贸通有无；荷畚执筐，各安职业。”这说明1,000多年前，畚、筐等竹制品已在安溪流行。明清时期，安溪竹藤编艺人不断增多，工艺水平不断提升。民国至今，竹藤编遍布安溪农村，成为百姓的家庭生计或副业。

在安溪，竹藤编生活用具相当普遍，有箧箍、筛、笼、篱、灯等14类40多个品种。竹藤编的工艺有多复杂，安溪人的手就有多巧。安溪竹藤编承袭唐代以来的编织法，在世人看来不起眼的山间植物，诸如毛竹、木料、海南藤、龙须藤、猫儿藤、本地山藤等等，再也寻常不过，可加上各色染料、清油，在本土手工艺师傅的手中，愣是编织出令人惊艳的各种花样来。

安溪竹藤编作品。（王柏峰 摄）
A piece of Anxi bamboo and rattan weaving work. (Photo by Wang Baifeng)

Anxi Bamboo and Rattan Weavings

Hollow inside, the tall, straight and beautiful bamboo has always been a favorite of Chinese scholars and artists. It is a metaphor of vitality and longevity, which usually relates to a gentleman who has exemplary conduct and noble character. Bamboo is planted in many places in China, but Anxi County is the only one that boasts 150,000 people involved in the bamboo weaving industry and won the titles of "China Rattan Iron Craft Capital" and "World Craft City for Rattan Iron Works", the latter of which was awarded by World Crafts Council.

Anxi is a county in the west of Quanzhou known for its oolong tea, Tieguanyin. As early as in the late Tang Dynasty, bamboo and rattan weaving was popular here. As could be seen from *Anxi Local Gazetteer in the Early Five Dynasties*, baskets and other bamboo products were prevalent in Anxi more than a thousand years ago. During the Ming and Qing dynasties, the number of bamboo and rattan weavers kept increasing and significant progress was made in their craftsmanship. Ever since the period of the Republic of China, bamboo and rattan weaving has become a household livelihood or side job for local populace in Anxi County.

In Anxi, bamboo and rattan utensils are quite common. There are altogether 14 categories and 40 varieties, including hoops, sieves, steamers, fences and lamps. The complicated weaving processes best demonstrate the ingenuity of Anxi people. The weaving method of Anxi bamboo and rattan products has been handed down from the Tang Dynasty. Unremarkable plants in the mountains such as bamboo, trees and all kinds of rattan are woven, dyed and varnished before the magic hands of the weavers turn them into a variety of amazing products.

“经纬有度，才是灵魂。”安溪竹藤编的编织花样可谓丰富多彩：除了十字编、人字编、六角编、螺旋编、圆面编、纹丝编这 6 类普通编织法，还有穿篾编、穿丝编、弹花、插筋、硬板花、花箍、结、画面编这 8 类特殊编织法，以及收束和夹口技法。

安溪人刮起的这股“竹林风”早在 1962 年就蜚声国外。当时出身于竹藤编世家的陈清河，主持设计制作了 30 件竹藤编工艺品，作为刘少奇主席出访东欧时携带的国家礼品，展示了安溪竹藤编的魅力。

20 世纪 70 年代以来，安溪竹藤编在传承核心技艺的基础上进行改进发展，完善了花筋、粘贴、染色、漂白等技巧，充分发扬刻、磨、染、贴等技术特长，使产品造型更加精致美观，千姿百态。1972 年，安溪竹藤编作品亮相全国工艺美术展览，其中《菠萝罐》入选《中国工艺美术》大型画册。1984 年，由安溪尚卿竹编工艺厂创作的《百花瓶》被评为福建省工艺美术“百花奖”省优质产品。

安溪师傅实在太擅长用指尖和竹藤“谈恋爱”，若非爱到极致，怎会使得一件件日用品出落得如此精致耐用。细看来，瓶、盘、篮、盒、罐、盆套，每一样竹藤器具，都是大道至简的回归。蓦然回首，今日美学家们提倡的日常生活审美化，其实早在千年以前，已被安溪人了然于胸，自发实践。

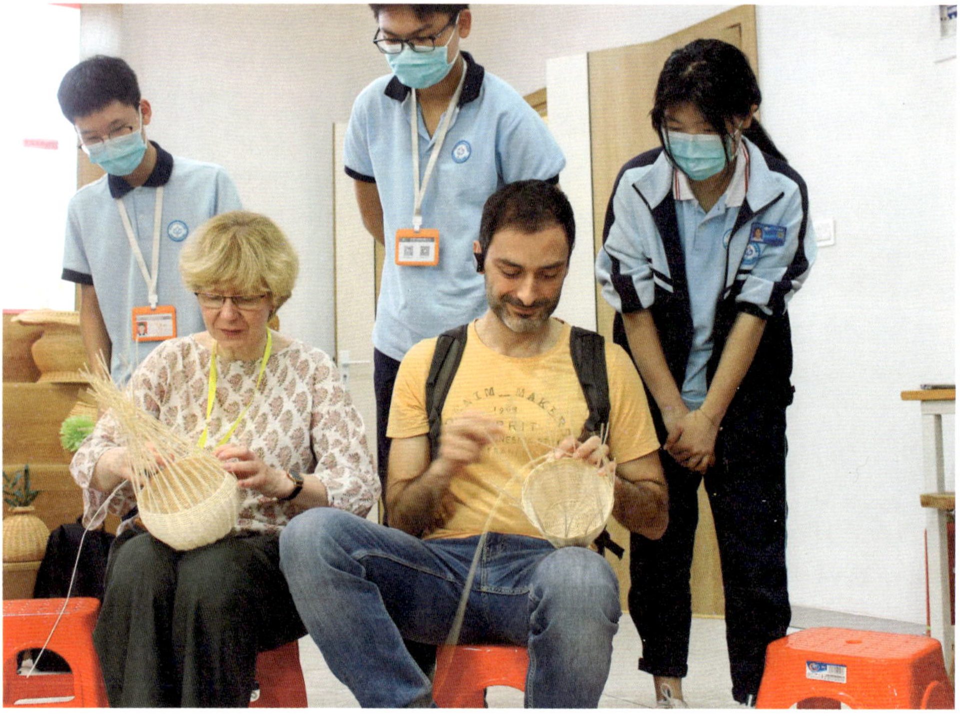

外宾在安溪华侨职业中专学校体验竹藤编制作。（易子明 摄）
Foreign visitors had a hands-on experience on Anxi Bamboo and Rattan Weavings at Anxi Vocational Secondary School. (Photo by Yi Ziming)

Patterns are the soul of weaving products. The patterns of bamboo and rattan weavings in Anxi are rich and colorful. In addition to the six common knitting methods, namely cross knitting, herringbone knitting, hexagonal knitting, spiral knitting, round knitting and stripe knitting, there are also eight special knitting methods, namely piercing, threading, springing, inserting skeletons, hard board knitting, flower hoops, knots and picture knitting, as well as the techniques of binding and clamping.

As early as in 1962, Chen Qinghe, who was born in a family of bamboo and rattan weaving craft, designed and made 30 bamboo and rattan works which were taken as gifts to the east European countries when the then president of China, Liu Shaoqi, visited them. And that was probably the debut of Anxi weaving products abroad.

Since the 1970s, Anxi craftsmen have been improving and developing the core bamboo weaving skills, perfecting techniques such as patterning, pasting, dyeing and bleaching. Through carving, grinding, dyeing and pasting, the products are more varied and delicate. In 1972, Anxi bamboo and rattan works appeared in the National Arts and Crafts Exhibition, and the picture of *Pineapple Pot* was selected into the pictorial encyclopedia, *Chinese Arts and Crafts*. In 1984, the *Hundred Flowers Vase* created by Anxi Shangqing Bamboo Weaving Craft Factory was recognized as a quality product of Fujian Province and won the "Hundred Flowers Award of Fujian Arts and Crafts".

It takes devotion and commitment to make utensils so exquisite and durable as Anxi bamboo weaving products. The bottles, plates, baskets, boxes, pots and pot holders all seem to reveal to us that the simplest is the prettiest and we may easily find that the life styles we advocate now, be it minimalist or eco-friendly, have been the usual way of life for Anxi people for more than a thousand years.

泉州木雕：
泉郡名匠，善雕浮屠花卉

“每一块木头，都在诉说。”见识过泉州木雕的人，总忍不住想猜透，那千刨万凿中一声不吭的缄默是来自怎样一种力量，才能忍受倾泻而下的刻刀，最终释放禁锢已久的木讷，成就永恒的灵动。

自唐以来，泉州就被称作“临海佛国”，在相当长的时间里，佛像是当地雕刻艺术的主要题材，与建筑雕刻相辅相成，流传至今。泉州木雕在宋元时期进入成熟期，据惠安发现的《鉴湖张氏族谱》记载，南宋张仕逊（1206—1291）于公元1236年参与重建开元寺大雄宝殿，其时雕刻的24尊飞天乐伎木雕是泉州现存最早的木雕上品，万千仪态，令人叹为观止。《鉴湖张氏族谱》还记载，张仲哥（1123—1194）为“泉郡名匠，善雕浮屠花卉，晋（江）南（安）同（安）宫阙泰半着手”，可见泉州木雕有文献记载的历史最迟可追溯至宋代。

Quanzhou Wood Carvings

Every piece of wood seems to have its own story to tell. People who have ever seen Quanzhou Wood Carvings cannot help but wonder at the magical hands that make the lifeless pieces of wood so lifelike.

Since the Tang Dynasty, Quanzhou has been a famous Buddhist resort by the sea. For quite a long time, Quanzhou Wood Carvings have been dominated by Buddha statues and supplemented by architectural sculptures. Quanzhou Wood Carvings matured during the Song and Yuan dynasties. According to the records of *Jianhu Zhang Clan Genealogy* discovered in Hui'an County, when Kaiyuan Temple was rebuilt in 1236 during the Song Dynasty, Zhang Shixun (1206—1291), a carving artist from today's Hui'an County, carved the 24 Flying Apsaras around the ceiling of the main hall, which are the earliest extant top-grade wood carvings in Quanzhou and whose myriad of manners are breathtaking. And documented also in the clan genealogy is Zhang Zhongge (1123—1194), a famous artisan in Quanzhou who was good at carving relief flowers and undertook the wood carving tasks for half of the temples in Jinjiang, Nan'an and Tong'an. Therefore, the documented history of Quanzhou Wood Carvings can be traced back to the Song Dynasty at the latest.

开元寺大雄宝殿飞天乐伎木雕。（陈英杰 摄）
Wood carvings of Flying Apsaras in the main hall of Kaiyuan Temple in Quanzhou. (Photo by Chen Yingjie)

虽由人作，宛自天开。泉州木雕仿佛泉州人吟唱的南音，气韵生动，妙手天成。代代相传的木雕技艺，在选材、工艺、题材、艺术风格等方面都已发展成熟，形成了一套独特完整的技艺体系。泉州港成为“东方第一大港”以后，泉州木雕精品在海外华侨和商人的呵护下，沿着海上丝绸之路漂洋过海，走向东南亚乃至全世界。

在无涯的时光洪流里，于千万人的供奉之中，固化而失落的木头，终究会等到要等的人。泉州木雕人才辈出、大师频现，无论是传统还是创新，十指灵动之间，都流淌着匠人们对自然恩赐的珍视和巧思。泉州木雕艺术大师卢思立曾说，木雕是做减法的艺术，在创作自然型木雕时，要先读懂木头，思考的过程往往比创作过程还长；假如立意不对，一刀下去，就会将独一无二的材料给破坏了。

天地有大美，且何其幸运，可在泉州匠师们的刀口间一一呈现。

中国工艺美术大师、省级非物质文化遗产代表性传承人卢思立（左一）正在创作中。（陈英杰 摄）
Lu Sili (first from left), Master of Chinese Arts and Crafts and Representative Inheritor of Fujian Intangible Culture Heritage, is carving. (Photo by Chen Yingjie)

Vivid and charming, Quanzhou Wood Carvings, akin to its Nanyin Music, look like the unique artworks of nature. In Quanzhou, the art of wood carvings passing down from generation to generation has matured in terms of material selection, craftsmanship, subject matter and artistic style. When Quanzhou became the largest port in the East during the Song and Yuan dynasties, merchants and some overseas Chinese began to sell its wood carvings to countries along the Maritime Silk Road.

Through hundreds of years, the age-old wood carvings of Quanzhou are beaming with new vitality. Be it traditional or innovative, works of wood carvings best illustrate the gift and ingenuity of masters' hands from different generations. Lu Sili, a master of wood carvings in Quanzhou, once said that wood carving is the art of subtraction, and that when creating a wood carving, one must first read the wood, and the design takes longer than the carving. If the design is faulty, a single cut will destroy the unique material.

Beauty is everywhere in our life and how lucky it is that it can be presented to us through the carving knives of Quanzhou craftsmen.

"世遗泉州 海丝文创"第三届泉州市文化创意产品展暨传统工艺美术精品展上的泉州木雕作品——《涨海声中万国商》。（视觉中国 供图）

Merchants from All Nations Thronged to Quanzhou Amidst the Sound of Rising Tides, a Quanzhou wood carving work presented at the Third Quanzhou Cultural and Creative Products Exhibition & Traditional Arts and Crafts Exhibition. (Courtesy of VCG.COM)

传统技艺：
敢称南派，惊为神力叹天工

Traditional Craftsmanship

闽南传统民居营造技艺：闽南古厝蔚大观，蔡杨民居比宫廷

Architectural Craftsmanship of Traditional Residence in Minnan (Southern Fujian)

水密隔舱福船制造技艺：国之重器，郑和下西洋指定用船

Watertight-Bulkhead Technology of Chinese Junks

德化瓷烧制技艺：海丝瓷，天下白；朝宗出，谁争锋

Firing Techniques of Dehua Porcelain

磁灶窑陶瓷烧制技艺：梯行万国，泉州匠心

Firing Techniques of Cizao Kilns

安溪铁观音制作技艺：舌根轻转观音韵，海外闻得圣妙香

Producing Techniques of Tieguanyin Oolong Tea in Anxi County

永春香制作技艺：海丝风帆携芳魂，重拾香道赢芳心

Producing Techniques of Yongchun Incense

闽南传统民居营造技艺：闽南古厝蔚大观，蔡杨民居比宫廷

它雄视板正严谨的北方四合院，笑傲纤弱温吞的江南白墙青瓦房。众声喧哗的年代，当钢筋水泥的丛林不断蚕食空间，它也只是报以拈花微笑，甘与岁月同寂。这般无意的洒脱，兀自矗立成南国建筑的独特风景线，正应和了存在主义大师海德格尔的那句名言——诗意地栖息在大地上。

闽南传统民居，一部生动的建筑学教科书，靠近者无不提高其建筑技艺认知的海拔。这是中原文化、本土文化和海洋文化融合的产物。南宋皇室南外宗迁入泉州后，把皇家宫殿建筑技艺带入泉州民间。于是，融合当地地理、气候特点和文化习俗而成的一种独特的建筑风格诞生了，并逐渐成为闽南地区古建筑行业的主流，常见于闽南文化圈的泉州、漳州、厦门，港澳台，以及东南亚地区。

严格说来，闽南传统民居包括泉州府的“几间张几落大厝”、漳州府的“爬狮”与“四点金”，以及闽南传统街市中的“手巾寮”。而泉州民居中最为典型的建筑俗称“皇宫起”，这种宫殿式大厝在泉州侨乡随处可见，有单护厝、双护厝、四护厝等类型和三开间、五开间等样式。“皇宫起”横向扩展布局，纵深有二落、三落、五落不等，它以庭院为组织单元，以走廊、过水贯穿全宅，建筑中较多运用砖、瓦，常以石砌基础和红砖砌筑外围墙，以穿斗木构架作承重结构，多采用硬山式屋顶和弯曲起翘的燕尾脊。

闽南传统民居典型的燕尾脊。（陈英杰 摄）
The typical upturned swallow-tailed eave of a traditional folk residence in Southern Fujian. (Photo by Chen Yingjie)

Architectural Craftsmanship of Traditional Residence in Minnan (Southern Fujian)

Just as Martin Heidegger, the German existentialist, put it, "Poetry builds up the very nature of dwelling." Minnan traditional residence is a case in point. Rivaling its counterparts, the quadrangle courtyard in Beijing and the white-walled, blue-tiled houses in the south of the Yangtze River, it stands out in the jungle of concrete with grace and ease.

Traditional residence in Southern Fujian is a textbook of architecture that promises enrichment for anyone who is interested. It is an integration of Central Plain culture, Southern Fujian culture and marine culture. In the Southern Song Dynasty, when descendants of the imperial clan migrated to Quanzhou, they brought with them architectural skills of the royal palaces, which, after being adapted to the local geography, climate and cultural conventions, evolved into a unique architectural style prevailing in the building of folk houses in Southern Fujian and later spread to regions like Hong Kong, Macao, Taiwan and some Southeast Asian countries.

Strictly speaking, traditional residence in Southern Fujian includes Dacuo (houses with several room-widths and sections) in Quanzhou, Pashi (a central building with two wings attached) and Sidianjin (the quadrangle courtyard) in Zhangzhou and Shoujinliao (the residence with a shop in the front) in street markets of Southern Fujian. But the most typical building in Quanzhou is called Huanggongqi (the official-type mansion), which is commonly seen in this famous hometown of overseas Chinese. An official-type mansion is either three-room wide or five-room wide with one, two or four wings. With two, three, five or more sections, it is built in line with the architectural style of imperial palaces, which has a symmetrical layout around a central courtyard with corridors and gutters round the whole residence. Beside the bricks and tiles frequently used in the building, a stone foundation and red brick masonry are used to build the outer walls, and through-jointed wood frames are used as the load bearing structure, while the roofs are gabled with upturned swallow-tailed eaves.

“皇宫起”为官式大厝，在全国民居建筑中绝无仅有。相传五代十国时期，闽王王审知因皇后黄惠姑的家乡（今惠安县张坂镇后边村）滨海风烈，老屋“日出十八天窗，雨来十八漏孔”，恩赐“汝母厝皇宫起”，即特许其按皇宫的规制和外形在家乡大兴土木，兴建住宅。然而由于在泉州本地话中，“汝母”和“汝府”的发音相近，这样就使得恩赐“皇宫起”的范围由黄皇后娘家一家，扩大到泉州一府，当地人争相仿效，建房兴宅，形成了千百年来泉州地区别致典雅、富丽堂皇的皇宫式古民居建筑，并流传到闽南文化圈的其他地区。

传奇之建筑，必出传奇之行家；传奇之建筑师，非惠安匠师莫属。惠安传统建筑历史悠久，文化积淀深厚，起自晋唐，兴于唐宋，明清两代进入鼎盛。闽地多兴宫庙寺院，惠安工匠的身影屡屡活跃其间，更有甚者，还渡海参与台湾地区乃至东南亚一些国家的寺庙营建。至清末民初，已是名师鹊起、精品迭出。中华人民共和国成立后，惠安建筑产业更是异彩焕发，成为闽南地区古建筑行业的龙头。

2009 年，由中国艺术研究院建筑研究所负责申报的中国传统木结构建筑营造技艺入选联合国教科文组织《人类非物质文化遗产代表作名录》。该项目由徽派传统民居营造技艺、北京四合院传统营造技艺、香山帮传统建筑营造技艺、闽南传统民居营造技艺捆绑申报。被誉为“闽南古厝大观”“世界建筑重要遗迹”的南安蔡氏古民居建筑群、鲤城杨阿苗民居荣列中国传统木结构建筑营造技艺范本；南安林氏民居、英都坂埔古厝、石井中宪第等亦被列为全国重点文物保护单位。

蔡氏古民居的红砖墙。（陈英杰 摄）
The red brick wall of the Cai Family's Ancient Residential Complex. (Photo by Chen Yingjie)

The official-type residence is unique nationwide. Legend has it that, during the Five Dynasties and Ten Kingdoms period (907—960), Wang Shenzhi, the vassal king of the Min Kingdom granted his queen, Huang Huigu, a native of Zhangban in today's Hui'an County, permission to build her parents' house modeling the palace as their old one was so badly designed that it was neither heat-resistant nor weatherproof. However, as the pronunciation of "your parents' house" is similar to that of "your parents' prefecture" in the local dialect, the building of houses patterning the palace extended from the queen's maiden family to the whole of Quanzhou and later to places where Southern Fujian dialect is spoken, thus forming a unique, elegant and magnificent palace-style of folk houses.

The building of these magnificent folk houses fostered a large number of great architects in Hui'an. Starting in the Jin and Tang dynasties and flourishing in the Tang and Song dynasties, Hui'an traditional architecture reached its peak in the Ming and Qing dynasties. The building of religious temples has been very popular in Southern Fujian and most of them are also the works of Hui'an architects, who were even invited to the Taiwan region and some Southeast Asian countries to help the construction of temples there. And there emerged a great many famous architects and architectural masterpieces in the late Qing and early Republican period. Hui'an construction industry reached new heights after the founding of the People's Republic of China and gradually dominates ancient architecture industry in Southern Fujian.

In 2009, the project, Chinese Traditional Architectural Craftsmanship for Timber-Framed Structures, which was submitted by the Institute of Architectural Art of Chinese Academy of Art, was inscribed on UNESCO's *Representative List of the Intangible Cultural Heritage of Humanity*. Included in the project are the craftsmanship for traditional architecture in Anhui, Beijing, Xiangshan of Suzhou and Southern Fujian. Displaying a panorama of Minnan architecture and hailed as the important relics of world architecture, the Cai Family's Ancient Residential Complex in Nan'an, the satellite city of Quanzhou, and the Former Residence of Yang Amiao in Licheng District of Quanzhou are listed as models of Chinese Traditional Architectural Craftsmanship for Timber-Framed Structures. While the Lin Family's Residence in Nan'an, Banpu Ancient Buildings in Yingdu Town and Zhongxiandi Official-Type Mansion in Shijing County are listed as major historical and cultural sites protected at the national level.

“皇宫起”宫殿式大厝就像一个聚落，承载着家族的繁衍生息，其“燕尾归脊”寓意燕子（子女）不管漂泊何地，不论路途多远，总要回归故里。这种观念在华侨中影响深远，成为海外侨胞认祖归宗、与祖国血脉相连而割裂不开的思乡情结，是维系中华民族千年血脉的精神纽带。如今，在闽南一些城市特色街区改造及新农村建设中，当地人也习惯采用传统民居营造技艺，新的建筑十分注重体现闽南建筑的风格，如红砖白石墙面装饰、燕尾脊等，这些都使得闽南传统建筑技艺得以延续和传承。

漫步大厝，如同行走在历史长廊，走过大门、明堂和天井，走过院落、书斋和戏台。如果走得再认真一些，你会走过尊严、体面和从容，继而走过晋、唐、明、清，走过岁月的宽窄。

此间共沐乡愁之约的伏笔，留给后来。

The official-type mansion is like a settlement, bearing the family heritage. And in the Chinese language, the swallow is usually used to symbolize children, so the swallow-tailed eaves imply a homeland love knot of the Chinese, namely, no matter where and how far the children travel, they will always return to their hometown. The idea has a far-reaching influence on the overseas Chinese and has become a spiritual bond that links the overseas Chinese, their ancestors and their homeland. It is this bond that maintains the root of the Chinese nation for thousands of years. Nowadays, in the renovation of some urban characteristic blocks and the construction of new rural areas in Southern Fujian, local people still favor the traditional style, such as the use of red bricks and white stone walls and the swallow-tailed eaves, hence enabling the continuation and inheritance of craftsmanship of traditional Minnan architecture.

Strolling around a big ancient folk house in Quanzhou is like walking in the corridor of history. You walk through the gate to the main hall and then the patio, the courtyard to the study and then the stage. You travel through the long years, from the Jin, the Tang, the Ming to the Qing Dynasty with dignity, grace and poise.

Then looking back, you know you are home and your root is here.

俯瞰蔡氏古民居。（陈起拓 摄）
An aerial view the Cai Family's Ancient Residential Complex. (Photo by Chen Qituo)

水密隔舱福船制造技艺：国之重器，郑和下西洋指定用船

公元 1405 年的第一场雪，比以往时候来得更早一些。

彼时的温陵泉州，虽一冬无雪，利刃般的朔风却凛冽地刮过刺桐港。一位身着锦袍的京官伫立在高大的龙船之上，吉时甫至，他一声令下，挥鞭直指沧海。扬帆，起锚，击水三千里，身后尾随的六十一艘宝船及其他各种船只，似一条巨龙，在东南海域掀起一道道水帘。

中国乃至世界航海史的最动人一幕，由此开启。

多年以后，历史学家给这场伟大的壮举定名为“郑和下西洋”。而那些乘风破浪的巨船的建造工程师们也有了一个集体的名字——泉州师傅。当时的船队忠武尉是长乐人李参，因着他的力荐，负责本次造船工程的闽派船帮第一次进入大明王朝皇家视线。帝国的荣耀在下西洋的无尽航程中，远播海内外，而福建泉州造船业技术也自此有了皇家的顶级背书。

时光来到清顺治十三年（1656），走上技艺巅峰的泉州造船业再次登上历史舞台。这一次是郑成功东征台湾，泉州福船又一次出色地完成了任务，以黄都公为首的黄氏造船工匠，凭借东方技术助力郑氏舰队打败初兴的资本主义强国——“海上马车夫”荷兰。数年后，康熙皇帝派施琅将军攻打台湾郑氏水军，战船成为促进祖国统一的国之重器。

郑和宝船模型。（视觉中国 供图）
A model of Zheng He's treasure ship. (Courtesy of VCG.COM)

Watertight-Bulkhead Technology of Chinese Junks

The first snow in 1405 came a little earlier than usual in China.

It was a snowless winter in Quanzhou, but the wind blew bitterly across the port of Zayton (another name for ancient Quanzhou). A royal official in a brocade robe stood atop a junk ship and when the right time came, he pointed his whip straight at the sea to order his fleet to set sail. Then, with sails raised, anchors heaved up and water splashed high, the ship, with the other sixty-one treasure ships and all kinds junks trailing behind, advanced like a giant dragon lifting curtains of water in the southeast sea of China.

Here came the most exciting moment in the maritime history of China and even the world.

Years later, historians named this great feat "Zheng He's voyages to the western oceans" and those who constructed the huge ships were also given a collective name—Quanzhou masters. Thanks to the recommendation of Li Can, a native of Changle, Fuzhou, who was then one of the leaders of the fleets, the shipbuilders of Southern Fujian had the first chance to be responsible for the royal shipbuilding project of the Ming Dynasty. The seven voyages of Zheng He demonstrated the glory of the Ming Dynasty far and wide. At the same time, Quanzhou shipbuilding technology received its top royal endorsement.

In 1656 during the Qing Dynasty, Quanzhou shipbuilding industry made a return appearance. Shipwrights of Quanzhou headed by Master Huang Dugong were hired to build warships which later enabled Zheng Chenggong's expulsion of the Dutch colonists, known as the Sea Coachman, from Taiwan. And decades later, when Emperor Kangxi of the Qing Dynasty sent General Shi Lang to attack Zheng's army to recover Taiwan, the warships played a very important part in promoting the reunification of China.

世人蹊跷于泉州福船的奥秘，此船的硬核技术到底是什么？为何一再成为同时代领先世界、降维打击对手的利器？清嘉庆年间蔡永蒹所撰《西山杂志 · 王尧造舟》提供了一条解读路径："天宝中，王尧于勃泥运来木材为林銮造舟。舟之身长十八丈……银镶舱舷十五格，可贮货品二至四万担之多。"这段重要的史料揭示了福船的一项核心技术——十五格，即后世所谓十五个隔舱。

隔舱，专业术语叫作水密隔舱，该技术的安全指数之高，使得中国的远洋木帆船早在宋元时期就称霸海上。西方人第一次知道原来中国帆船有这样独特的结构：船舱中，以横隔板分隔出彼此独立且不透水的一个个舱区；每个单独的舱区都由隔舱板、船壳板、水底板、船甲板围成，构成相对独立的空间；隔舱板的位置与隔舱的尺寸大小及舱的用途密切相关，另外还要考虑到船舶的结构强度；隔舱板一般设置在船壳板弯曲的拐点处，用以支撑船壳板，从而增加船体的强度与刚度。这种结构的优势在于，当一个船舱遇到意外破损时，其他船舱不受影响，能保证行船安全，且便于修复。还有很重要的一点是，隔舱板横向支撑船舷，增强了船体抵御侧向水压和风浪的能力。

明代《三才图会》中的福船，船舱是水密隔舱结构。（视觉中国 供图）

A Fu-Chuan built with the watertight bulkhead technology appeared in *Collected Illustrations of the Three Realms*, the Ming Dynasty encyclopedia by Wang Qi and his son Wang Siyi, published in 1609. (Courtesy of VCG.COM)

Why is it that junks made in Quanzhou, or Fu-Chuan, were so tough? What is the hardcore technology? An interpretation could probably be found in the book *Xishan Miscellaneous Records* about Southern Fujian written by Cai Yongjian, a Quanzhou scholar in the Qing Dynasty. According to the book, in the middle of the Tang Dynasty, Wang Yao brought timber from Brunei, an ancient Asian kingdom in the northern part of Kalimantan, to build a ship for Lin Luan, a noted navigator and merchant in Dongshi, Quanzhou. The silver inlaid cabin had 15 compartments and could carry cargoes of one to two million kilograms. Mystery solved. The 15 compartments are watertight and the key technology is now known as the watertight-bulkhead technology of Fu-Chuan.

Compartments, technically called watertight bulkheads, provide technology that made China's ocean-going wooden sailboats dominate the sea as early as in the Song and Yuan dynasties. Westerners knew for the first time that Chinese sailboats had such a unique structure: the compartments are separated from each other by horizontal bulkheads; each separate cabin area is composed of the bulkhead, the shell plating, the waterproof bottom plate and the ship decks, forming a relatively independent space; the position of the bulkhead is closely related to the size and purpose of the compartment as well as the structural strength of the ship; bulkheads are generally set at the bends of the shell plating to support it, thereby increasing the strength and rigidity of the ship. The advantage of this construction is that when one compartment is accidentally damaged, the other compartments are not affected, thus ensuring safety and facilitating repair. Equally important is that the horizontal bulkheads support the sides and increase the shell's ability to resist lateral water pressure from the wind and waves.

一般而言，船只越大，其隔舱就越多，载客为主的船舶会比货船有更多的水密隔舱。在闽南地区，隔舱板被称为母营、堵营、堵壁或堵板等，因此，帆船又有三母营、七母营、九母营之说。水密隔舱福船从船型到浑然流畅的曲线设计，都充分保留与体现了古福船的特点，其形式对现代船只功能美学及设计艺术有一定的研究借鉴意义。

13 世纪末，意大利人马可·波罗初见此技，遂马不停蹄地将其介绍到西方。大约 500 年后的 1795 年，英国海军总工程师塞缪尔·本瑟姆把这项技术首次用于建造新型军舰。自此，水密隔舱技术开始在各国造船界普及，开启了人类航海史的新时代。

2010 年，联合国教科文组织确认中国水密隔舱福船制造技艺列入《急需保护的非物质文化遗产名录》。

蓝天和大海平行，归帆与月色同路。蹈海人的心里，有一座庙宇，叫作故乡。福船，泉州的，福建的，中国的，世界的！

泉州泉港峰尾造船厂工匠采用水密隔舱技艺，以 1∶1 的比例复原明代福船并成功下水航行。（陈小阳 摄）
The shipwrights of Fengwei Shipyard in Quangang District of Quanzhou restored a Ming Dynasty Fu-Chuan with watertight bulkheads at a ratio of 1:1 and had it successfully launched. (Photo by Chen Xiaoyang)

In general, the larger the ship, the more compartments there will be and passenger ships feature more watertight compartments than cargo ships. In Southern Fujian, there are ships with three, seven or nine bulkheads. The watertight bulkheads of treasure ships made in Quanzhou have fully preserved and embodied the characteristics of ancient vessels from the shape to the smooth curve design and can be used for reference to the making and design of modern ships.

In the late 13th century, Marco Polo, the Venetian merchant, explorer and writer who traveled through Asia along the Silk Road between 1271 and 1295, introduced this technology to the West soon after he knew it. Some five hundred years later, in 1795, Samuel Bentham, chief engineer of the British Navy, first applied this technology to build a new type of warship. Since then, the watertight-bulkhead technology began to popularize in the shipbuilding industry of various countries, ushering in a new era in the history of human navigation.

In 2010, the Watertight-Bulkhead Technology of Chinese Junks was inscribed on the *List of Intangible Cultural Heritage in Need of Urgent Safeguarding* by UNESCO.

For people who spend much of their life on the sea, there's a place they hold sacred in their hearts and it is called homeland. And home to the watertight-bulkhead technology, Quanzhou sees its vessels in the spotlight of Fujian, China and the world.

水密隔舱福船制造技艺传承人陈春来正在制作模型。（林劲峰 摄）
Chen Chunlai, an inheritor of the Watertight-Bulkhead Technology of Fu-Chuan, is making a model. (Photo by Lin Jinfeng)

德化瓷烧制技艺：海丝瓷，天下白；朝宗出，谁争锋

2017 年 11 月 27 日，在香港佳士得秋季拍卖会的“御苑 · 文心 · 匠艺——明代器物书画晚间拍卖”专场上，“明代瓷圣”何朝宗的德化窑白釉渡海观音立像以 1,600 万港元落槌。消息一出，业界哗然。世人在惊叹的同时，也自然而然地把目光聚焦在呈现这惊世之作的德化瓷身上。

瓷品的德化制造，业界有口皆碑。翻开德化这座小县城的履历，你会发现，它的头衔和关键词一直深深地烙着陶瓷的印记。作为中国陶瓷文化的发祥地和三大古瓷都之一，德化走过了数千载的造瓷春秋，最终成为全国最大的工艺瓷生产和出口基地、中国十大主要陶瓷产区之一。

一方水土孕育一方物产。德化坐拥“闽中屋脊”戴云山脉的中段主峰，亚热带季风气候又为其带来雨热的滋养，正可谓山多、水足、矿富，陶瓷生产所必备的燃料、水流和矿藏资源在其境内均可找到。

任何一地，能有大造化，光有老天爷的垂青可不行。德化瓷能够走到今天，不仅靠天时地利，更得靠“祖师爷赏饭吃”，代代相传的制瓷技艺，才是它恒久流传、睥睨天下的资本。

德化瓷烧制现场。（陈英杰 摄）
The scene of firing Dehua Porcelain. (Photo by Chen Yingjie)

Firing Techniques of Dehua Porcelain

On November 27, 2017, at Christie's Autumn Auction in Hong Kong, "Court, Studio, Atelier—Chinese Works of Art and Paintings from the Ming Dynasty Evening Sale", a statue of Guanyin (the God of Mercy) Crossing the Sea, made by He Chaozong, the most celebrated master potter of Dehua Porcelain in Quanzhou, Fujian in the Ming Dynasty, was auctioned at the price of HK$ 16 million. The news made headlines, and Dehua Porcelain came naturally under the spotlight.

Dehua is famous for its porcelain industry. Dig a little into its history and you'll easily find that ceramics has been an indispensable part of it. As the birthplace of Chinese ceramic culture and one of the three ancient porcelain capitals, Dehua has gone through thousands of years of porcelain making, and finally became the largest production and export base of ceramic artworks in China as well as one of the ten major ceramic producers in China.

Nature endows different places with different resources. The subtropical monsoon climate brings abundant rainfall and sunshine to Dehua, which is located at the foot of the main peak in the middle of Daiyun Mountains, the "roof of central Fujian". And the favorable geographic location and climate in turn provide the fuel, water and minerals necessary for ceramic production.

But nature's favor alone is not enough to bring prosperity. It is the art of porcelain making that makes Dehua exceptional.

窑炉内部。（陈英杰 摄）
The interior of a kiln. (Photo by Chen Yingjie)

思接千载，视通万里。德化瓷烧制技艺最早可追溯到新石器时代的印纹陶器烧造，到唐代德化已开始烧制青釉器。德化县内保存着宋元时期的碗坪和屈斗宫等窑址，宋代生产的白瓷和青瓷已很精致，并开始大量出口。元代，德化瓷塑佛像已用于进贡朝廷，得到帝王的赏识。明、清两代，德化瓷大量流传到欧洲，它的象牙白釉（又名奶油白）对欧洲的瓷器艺术产生过很大的影响。清代德化诗人郑兼才曾在《窑工》一诗中发出感慨：“一朝海舶来，顺流价倍蓰。不怕生计穷，但愿通潮水。”

何朝宗就是明代著名的德化瓷手艺人。他利用当地优质的高岭土，使用捏、塑、雕、刻、刮、削、接、贴八种技法制作出精美的德化瓷塑，釉色乳白，如脂如玉，格调素雅，为德化瓷赢得了“象牙白”“中国白”等美誉，使其成为中国白瓷的代表。郑和下西洋所带的瓷器中就有福建的德化瓷。意大利著名旅行家马可·波罗在游历福建泉州时，也盛赞德化陶瓷并将其带往海外各地。可以说，明代的德化制瓷技术已经达到历史最高水平，在造型艺术方面也达到前所未有的高度，成为陶瓷世界里天生丽质、别具一格的艺术作品。

一波波，一浪浪，无数德化工匠们，在世代的传承中，在岁月的更替中，默默地推动着德化瓷精益求精的创作，使其烧制技艺登顶华夏民窑巅峰，不落官窑窠臼，集实用性、装饰性、观赏性于一体，展现民间高手的超群智慧与艺术追求。

有人说瓷是修炼得道的玉，因泥塑形，以水调和，终于蹈火涅槃。德化瓷也一样，它甘于被揉捏、被煅烧，在几千度的高温中经受真火的考验，凡胎终究脱俗，成万物，成仙佛，成为超越本我的神品。

德化天下白，万圣属朝宗！

国家级非物质文化遗产代表性传承人陈明良正在创作。（郑锦昕 摄）
Chen Mingliang, Representative Inheritor of the National Intangible Cultural Heritage, is creating. (Photo by Zheng Jinxin)

The Firing Techniques of Dehua Porcelain can be traced back as far as the Neolithic era with the firing of stamped pottery, and by the Tang Dynasty the firing of celadon glazed ware had begun. Preserved in Dehua County today are kiln sites such as Wanping and Qudougong from the Song and Yuan dynasties, where delicate white and celadon porcelain was produced in the Song Dynasty and began to be exported in large quantities. During the Yuan Dynasty, porcelain statues of Buddhas from Dehua were already tributes to the imperial court and were much loved by the emperor. During the Ming and Qing dynasties, Dehua porcelain was spread widely to Europe, and its ivory white glaze (or cream white) had a great influence on the European porcelain art. Zheng Jiancai, a Dehua poet of the Qing Dynasty, commented in his poem, *Potters of the Kilns*, on the good price and the ready market that the porcelain of Dehua enjoyed.

He Chaozong, a distinguished Dehua ceramic master of the Ming Dynasty, used the local high-quality kaolinite to produce exquisite Dehua Porcelain with eight techniques: kneading, moulding, sculpting, carving, scraping, chipping, piecing and pasting. The porcelain sculptures he made were known as "ivory white" or "Blanc de Chine" (White from China) for their lard white glaze looked like jade and the style was simple and elegant. Among the ceramics Zheng He brought to the West was Dehua Porcelain from Fujian. When the famous Italian traveler Marco Polo traveled to Quanzhou, Fujian, he also praised Dehua Porcelain and brought them overseas. It's safe to say that Dehua Porcelain firing techniques had reached the peak in the Ming Dynasty and the art of modeling had also reached an unprecedented height, making it a unique work of art in the world of ceramics.

Through the years, generations of Dehua potters keep perfecting themselves while absorbing the craftsmanship from their predecessors, hence making their firing techniques of porcelain the pinnacle of Chinese folk kilns. Different from the imperial porcelain, Dehua products are unique and original in that besides display porcelain and artistic porcelain, there is also daily used chinaware, which best embodies the outstanding wisdom and artistic pursuit of the folk masters.

Some compare porcelain to processed jade. Mixed with water and shaped out of pieces of white clay, they are kneaded and then burned in a temperature of several thousand degrees Celsius before they are finally transformed into art treasures.

Blanc de Chine is also Blanc du monde. White from Dehua is white from China and white from China is also "Treasure of the World".

何朝宗塑白瓷观音像。（成冬冬 摄）

A white porcelain statue of Guanyin by He Chaozong, the most celebrated master potter of Dehua. (Photo by Cheng Dongdong)

金砖国家领导人厦门会晤国家礼品、苏献忠德化瓷作品——《五音和鸣》。（郑永集 摄）
The state gift for BRICS Xiamen Summit, Five Tones in Harmony, a Dehua Porcelain work by Su Xianzhong. (Photo by Zheng Yongji)

许瑞峰德化瓷作品——《双狮献瑞》。（许瑞峰 供图）
Twin Lions Offering Good Luck, a Dehua Porcelain work by Xu Ruifeng. (Courtesy of Xu Ruifeng)

磁灶窑陶瓷烧制技艺：梯行万国，泉州匠心

瓷器是古老中国汇通世界贸易的重要法门。商品与国名相同的背后，氤氲着一种技术崇拜与价值认同。

泉州本想低调，但实力却不允许。踽踽于 10 至 14 世纪的时间长河，它衔枚疾进，逐渐成为夜空中最亮的星，以 150 多处外销陶瓷窑遗址牢牢占据了当时中国窑址密度第一的地位，享誉国际的泉州磁灶窑更是此中翘楚。

磁灶窑陶瓷烧制技艺的孕育地磁灶镇位于泉州西南约 16 千米处的晋江市，其境内分布的古代窑址遗存有着共同或相似的历史与考古学文化内涵，因而被统一命名为“磁灶窑”。2006 年，磁灶窑址被国务院公布为第六批全国重点文物保护单位之一，2020 年被定为“泉州：宋元中国的世界海洋商贸中心”的出口商品生产代表性遗产点。磁灶窑的陶瓷烧制历史距今已有 1,500 多年，宋元时期，其产品外销到日本和东南亚诸国，是福建古代外销陶瓷的主产地之一。

当时的泉州港一骑绝尘，晋升为“东方第一大港”。当仁不让的贸易之风吹彻磁灶窑昼夜不息的炉火，战天斗地的生产力与亚热带季风一起，淬成了青、绿、黄、黑、酱等各种釉色，弥补了瓷土粗糙的不足，突出了匠人扬长避短的智慧；垫柱支烧，窑具凸显特色；海外定烧，以独一无二的伊斯兰风格缠枝纹和云纹，打磨极具个性的艺术造型。正所谓，尊重人类需求的珍品，才是大国匠心的态度。

磁灶窑（金交椅山）遗址。（黄国炎 摄）
Sites of Cizao Kilns (Jinjiaoyishan Kilns). (Photo by Huang Guoyan)

Firing Techniques of Cizao Kilns

China, a high quality porcelain, starts the overseas trade of ancient China. The same name used for a commodity as well as the nation where it is produced is no doubt a recognition for the techniques and an expression of shared values.

With 150 or more export-porcelain kiln sites constructed between the 10th and 14th century, Quanzhou ranked first in the number of kilns then in China, among which Cizao Kilns came top.

Cizao Kilns are located in Cizao Town, 16 kilometers southwest of Quanzhou City. The kilns dotting its territory are uniformly named "Cizao Kilns" as they share common or similar historical and archaeological features. In 2006, the sites of Cizao Kilns were included into the sixth batch of major historical and cultural sites protected at the national level by the State Council of China. In 2020, they were designated as the representative heritage sites for the production of export commodities of Quanzhou, Emporium of the World in Song-Yuan China. The history of Cizao Kilns can be traced back to over 1,500 years ago. And during the Song and Yuan dynasties, Cizao wares were exported to Japan and Southeast Asian countries, making Cizao Kilns one of the main producers of export porcelain in ancient Fujian.

During that period, Quanzhou became the largest port in the East and Cizao saw the export of its ceramics surged and a great many kilns were constructed. As the raw materials used to make porcelain wares in Cizao were coarse and loose, the clever potters took advantage of the subtropical monsoon climate and coated the wares with engobe to make them finer by glazing them blue, green, yellow, black or brown. Cizao products won a competitive edge by developing their own style and catering to different demands of the overseas market, among which the most popular ones are porcelain with typical Islamic interlaced floral patterns and cloud patterns. Isn't this a kind of ingenuity with an open mind?

而今日念兹在兹的全球化，早在中世纪的磁灶窑产品中，就得以生动演绎。近年来，在频频发现于东海、南海的沉船中，著名的“南海Ⅰ号”“华光礁Ⅰ号”上都有大量磁灶窑产品出水。颇让世人感佩的是，出落得如此精致的瓷器，并不因其“订单式”批量需求而质量下降，常有精品妍态袭人，令人眼前一亮。磁灶窑陶瓷，堪称宋元泉州以海外贸易为中心的独特经济形态之生动样本。

磁灶窑陶瓷烧制技艺工艺娴熟，表现手法多样，作品洋溢着民间生活气息和乡土韵味，在器形、纹饰上反映出适应海外市场需求的风格，显现出中国陶瓷发源地之一和中国重要外销陶瓷产地弥足珍贵的历史价值。磁灶窑陶瓷烧制技艺及其遗址以及关联环境构成，见证了曾经的世界贸易大港泉州港的发展，体现了宋元泉州富有特色的海外贸易体系与多元社会结构，多维度地支撑了“宋元中国的世界海洋商贸中心”这一价值主题。

千年已降，你好，磁灶窑窑工！你的匠心，你的技艺，连同刺桐花的倩影，至今仍在天风海雨中熠熠生辉。

磁灶窑制品。（成冬冬 摄）
Products of Cizao Kilns. (Photo by Cheng Dongdong)

As early as in the Middle Ages, products of Cizao Kilns have demonstrated what globalization is. In recent years, a large number of products of Cizao Kilns came out of the sunken Song Dynasty merchant ships Nanhai No. 1 (South China Sea No. 1) and Huaguangjiao No. 1, two famous ones among the shipwrecks frequently found in the East China Sea and the South China Sea. What impresses the world is that these exquisite porcelain which were still elegant and eye-catching when salvaged were of superior quality despite the bulk orders and mass production at their time. The fine ceramics of Cizao were the vivid sample of Song-Yuan Quanzhou's unique economic form, which centered on overseas trade.

The Firing Techniques of Cizao Kilns were highly skilled and well diversified. While fulfilling the daily needs of the local people, the wares of Cizao also catered to the overseas markets in the shape and decoration, revealing the historical value of Cizao as one of the birthplaces of Chinese ceramics and an important producer of export ceramics. The porcelain firing techniques, together with the kiln sites and relics of Cizao, witness the development of Quanzhou Port, once a world trade center, showcase the distinctive overseas trade system and the pluralistic social structure of Quanzhou in the Song and Yuan dynasties and serve as a testament to Quanzhou's value as a maritime emporium of the world during the Song and Yuan periods in China.

Over the thousands of years, Erythrina flowers are still in full bloom every spring while Cizao Kilns, the largest group of ancient kiln sites, attracts a great many visitors looking up to their super craftsmanship as before.

磁灶窑制品。（成冬冬 摄）
Products of Cizao Kilns. (Photo by Cheng Dongdong)

安溪铁观音制作技艺：
舌根轻转观音韵，海外闻得圣妙香

戴云山逶迤于东南的支脉，层峦叠嶂，低丘、高丘、低山、中山，河谷盆地，点缀于安溪大地。造物主便是安溪的“老铁”，他对这个挚友的偏爱，近乎宠溺。你看这里，泉甘土赤，朝雾夕岚，低温、高湿、多雾，以及 pH 在 4.0 到 5.5 之间的酸性土壤，一切都恰到好处。

留住春天，安溪人只需一双巧手。茶叶与指尖的舞蹈，便把人间绝品铁观音推向了世界茶叶舞台的中央。

观音有韵，其来有自。关于铁观音的缘起，有两个传说，至今仍在《安溪县志》铭刻。一是“魏说”。相传，清雍正三年（1725），西坪峣阳松林头（今西坪镇松岩村）有老茶农魏荫，信奉观音菩萨。一日得菩萨托梦，在观音仑打石坑发现一株奇异的茶树。他十分欢喜，遂将茶树移植至家中一口破铁鼎里，悉心培育，经数年压枝繁殖，适时采制，果然茶质特异，香韵非凡。既是因观音托梦而得，就称之为“铁观音”。二是“王说”。相传，西坪峣阳南岩（今西坪镇南岩村）仕人王士让，清乾隆元年（1736）告假回乡，在书轩旁南山见层石荒园间有株茶树异于他种，就移栽至书轩之圃，精心管理，采制成品，香馥味醇。乾隆六年（1741），王士让应召赴京，以此茶馈赠礼部侍郎方苞，后者品其味非凡，遂转献内廷。乾隆饮后甚喜，认为此茶乌润结实，沉重似“铁”，味香形美，犹如“观音”，便赐名“铁观音”。

安溪茶山（李子宏 摄）
A tea plantation in Anxi County (Photo by Li Zihong)

Producing Techniques of Tieguanyin Oolong Tea in Anxi County

With low hills, high hills, low mountains, rugged mountains and river valley basins dotting the landscape, Anxi is favorably endowed by nature. The meandering Daiyun Mountains, the sweet springs and red sandstone soil, the mist, the low temperature and high humidity, the fog and the 4.0 to 5.5 PH value of the acidic soil all make it an ideal place for tea planting.

For people in Anxi, the dexterous fingers of theirs alone can make spring stay. Every spring, you'll see fingers dancing among the tea leaves and people busy making Tieguanyin (Iron God of Mercy) tea, one of China's most beloved oolong tea.

The origin of tree species and producing techniques that endow Tieguanyin tea with a special taste seemed to be interpreted in two legends recorded in *Anxi Local Gazetteer*. One is the legend about Wei Yin. In 1725 during the Qing Dynasty, Wei, an old tea farmer in Songlintou, Yaoyang, Xiping (now Songyan Village, Xiping Town) who believed in Guanyin Bodhisattva was inspired by the God in his dream and he found a rare tea tree in the stone pit of Guanyinlun. He was so happy that he transplanted it to a broken iron pod at home and cultivated it carefully. After several years of propagation, he picked it in time. As expected, the tea had a special quality and extraordinary fragrance. And as the tea was obtained under the guidance of Guanyin Bodhisattva, he named it Tieguanyin tea. The other legend is about Wang Shirang. In 1736 during the Qing Dynasty, Wang, an official from Nanyan, Yaoyang, Xiping (now Nanyan Village, Xiping Town) returned home for a holiday. Among the crevice of stones in the South Hill next to his study, he saw a tea tree different from the other species and transplanted it to the garden of his study. He cultivated it into a bush with leaves that produced a singularly fine drink. And then in 1741, Wang, after returning to the capital by the emperor's edict, presented the tea as a gift to Fang Bao, the vice minister of rites who raved about it and sent it as a tribute to Emperor Qianlong. The emperor, a tea connoisseur, was so impressed with the tea. He thought the leaves were dark as iron (*tie*, dialect of Southern Fujian for iron) and heavier than other tea, the taste was strong and mellow, and the look was as pure and beautiful as Guanyin Bodhisattva. Therefore, he granted it the name "Tieguanyin".

传说归传说，说法不一，不足为奇；好茶拼技艺，那才叫冠绝一方！

安溪铁观音的制作技艺是中国所有茶类中最独特的。清雍正年间，安溪茶农参考红茶全发酵和绿茶不发酵的制茶原理，结合铁观音的实际，创造出一套半发酵的独特制茶工艺，并根据不同的季节、气候、茶叶鲜度等灵活运用“看青做青”和“看天做青”技术。其主要制作方法是：通过人为控制和调节，经晒青、凉青、摇青，使茶青发生一系列物理、生物、化学变化，形成奇特的“绿叶红镶边”现象和独特的色、香、味内质，再以高温杀青制止酶的活性，最后进行揉捻和反复多次的包揉、烘焙，形成带有天然兰花香和独特“观音韵”的高雅品质。

虽据深山中，茶香飘万里。千年以后的今天，安溪铁观音再度扬帆，踏上“新丝路”，除了远销日本、东南亚等传统海外销区外，还西渐欧盟各国和美国，北上俄罗斯，不仅频频刷新海外出口的新纪录，更从低单价制品走向中高端定制的模式，让越来越多的外国友人深深地迷恋上安溪铁观音，爱上中国茶文化。

2022 年 2 月 27 日 11 时 06 分，在文昌卫星发射中心，“安溪铁观音一号”卫星成功搭载“长征八号”遥二运载火箭发射升空，该卫星是世界上第一颗以茶叶名冠名的遥感卫星。

人与安溪茶的故事，仍在演绎。茶和安溪人的宿缘，终无尽时。

老厝晒新茶。（陈英杰 摄）
Drying fresh tea leaves on the roof-top of an old house. (Photo by Chen Yingjie)

It is not at all surprising that there are many versions of legends. However, the proof of a good tea is in its techniques of producing.

Anxi Tieguanyin is the most unique among all kinds of Chinese tea in terms of the making process. Between 1723 and 1735 during the Qing Dynasty, having learned from the principles of full fermentation of black tea and non-fermentation of green tea, Anxi tea farmers created a unique tea making process of semi-fermented Tieguanyin, which adapted flexibly according to the weather, the variety and the growth of the tea. The producing techniques are as follows: through artificial control and regulation, have the tea leaves undergo a series of physical, biological and chemical changes through withering, cooling and tossing, bringing them with red edges and resulting in unique color, aroma and taste; then stop the enzymatic oxidation quickly while keeping the tea at its finest flavor with high temperature; roll the leaves to make them curly and give them a unique shape; dry the leaves to bring out its natural floral fragrance and unique taste.

Though made in a remote mountainous area, Tieguanyin enjoys a ready market abroad. With the revival of the Maritime Silk Road, the tea is sold to EU countries and the USA in the west and Russia in the north besides the traditional overseas markets of Japan and some Southeast Asian countries in the east. Export of the tea keep hitting new heights when more and more foreigners are mad about Anxi Tieguanyin and Chinese tea culture. And the tea is moving from a low-priced product to a medium- to high-end customized product.

At 11:06 on February 27, 2022, China's Long March-8 Y2 carrier rocket was launched from Wenchang Space Launch Center, carrying with it Anxi Tieguanyin No. 1 Satellite, the world's first remote sensing satellite named after tea.

The story of man and Anxi Tieguanyin is not yet finished for it has so much to offer.

永春香制作技艺：
海丝风帆携芳魂，重拾香道赢芳心

从哪里，才能追溯到一种气味的源头？一片海，依然在以流水的方式诉说着往事。

1974 年，一则考古信息轰动了全世界：一艘载重超过 200 吨的南宋远洋货船在泉州后渚港发掘出土。此次挖掘让无数奇珍异宝重见天日，其中一大批名贵香料的出现却成了不解之谜。

谁是这些香料的主人？它们从哪里来，又要到哪里去？为了揭开这个谜底，古船发现者之一、厦门大学历史系教授庄为玑数次深入泉州永春，寻找宋元之际盛极一时的泉州首富蒲氏家族的后人。凭借多年的研究经验，他敏锐地嗅到，此二者之间有着某种特殊的联系。

令世人不解的是，曾睥睨海上的蒲氏家族，为何会远在深山永春？

宋元时期，泉州刺桐港成功登顶“东方第一大港”，成为海上丝绸之路（又称“香料之路”）的起锚地。当时，定居泉州的阿拉伯后裔蒲寿庚家族拥有大量海船，一手垄断泉州香料海外贸易近三十年，富可敌国。

时过境迁，蒲氏家族经历种种打击，一落千丈。延至明清鼎革之际，闽南沿海大乱。清顺治三年（1646），蒲氏后人蒲世茂由晋江东石迁居永春卓埔后溪寨（现达埔镇汉口村），建古榕堂，成为永春蒲氏开基祖。蒲氏家族的传统产业香业也随之入永，在永春蒲家累世传承不辍。

远眺达埔。（康庆平 摄）
Overlooking the town of Dapu. (Photo by Kang Qingping)

Producing Techniques of Yongchun Incense

Where can we trace the source of a smell? The sea has a story to tell us with the flowing water.

In 1974, the news of an archaeological finding became a hit. An ocean-going cargo vessel of the Southern Song Dynasty with a load of over 200 tons was excavated in Houzhu Port, Quanzhou. Among the countless treasures unearthed, a large quantity of spices became a mystery.

Who was the owner of these spices? Where did they come from and where were they to be sent? To unravel this mystery, Zhuang Weiji, one of the discovers of the ancient ship as well as a professor of history from Xiamen University, went to Yongchun County in Quanzhou several times to look for the descendants of the Pu family, the richest family in Quanzhou during the Song and Yuan dynasties. With his years of experience in research, he sensed that there must have been a special connection between the two.

It is intriguing why the Pu family, the once tycoon of overseas trade should settle down in such a hinterland as Yongchun.

During the Song and Yuan dynasties, Zayton Harbor of Quanzhou became the largest port in the East, making Quanzhou the starting point of the Maritime Silk Road, also known as the Spice Route. At that time, the Pu Shougeng family, of Arab descent, who had settled in Quanzhou, owned a large number of sea vessels and monopolized the overseas trade of spices in Quanzhou for nearly thirty years, making themselves super rich.

As time passed, the Pu family gradually declined after going through various blows. During the transition from the Ming to the Qing Dynasty, the costal area of Southern Fujian was in turmoil. In 1646, led by Pu Shimao, some descendants of the Pu family moved from Dongshi in Jinjiang to settle down in Houxi Village, Zhuopu, Yongchun (now Hankou Village, Dapu Town). They built their clan hall called Gurongtang Hall there and Pu Shimao became the founding father of the Pu family in Yongchun. Came with them was the traditional incense business of the Pu family which has hereafter been passed down to their descendants in Yongchun for generations.

及至 1929 年，蒲氏在永春五里街西安路开设蒲庆兰香室，香料原料从厦门港进口，产品犹有宋元遗风，远销南洋群岛。1933 年，蒲庆兰香室在永春《崇道报》上刊登启事时提到：“本号历数世经验，所制各色名香，实超闽南。”蒲氏所言非虚，永春香制作极其讲究，它以本地几百种中药材为主料，遵古法制作，燃之香气独特，持久醇和，沁心入脑。纯天然的原材料和手工打磨使之锤炼出安神、养生、祛病的神奇功效，自古以来就是闽南人眼中上等香的代名词。

出自贵族世家的永春香在 2006 年成为国家地理标志保护产品。2014 年，中国轻工业联合会和中国日用杂品工业协会联合授予福建省永春县达埔镇“中国香都”称号。

香之为用大矣。德国作家聚斯金德在其名作《香水》中曾说：“谁掌握了气味，谁就掌握了人心。”在一众国际知名品牌精心炮制香味的时代，有一种东方香味，从未消失，朝觐着最古老的华贵与雍容。

“愿此香华云，遍满十方界。”

场面壮观的达埔晒香。（陈英杰 摄）
A spectacular scene of drying incense sticks in Dapu Town. (Photo by Chen Yingjie)

In 1929, Pu Qinglan Incense Store was opened in Xi'an Road, Wuli Street in Yongchun. The raw materials were imported via Xiamen Port while the products which were made with techniques inherited from the Song and Yuan dynasties, were sold to the Southeast Asian countries around the Malay Archipelago. In 1933, the store so advertised in a local newspaper, *Chongdao News*: With a long history of incense making, we boast the best products in Southern Fujian. That was true. With hundreds of local Chinese herbs as the main ingredients, the processing of Pu's incense, which follows the traditional techniques, is extremely elaborate and complicated. The product, when being burnt, gives out a unique, long-lasting, mellow and refreshing aroma. The pure natural ingredients together with hand crafting refine its magical effects of soothing the nerves, nourishing body and mind, and preventing illness, making it a byword for the finest incense in Southern Fujian since ancient times.

In 2006, Yongchun incense, with an aristocratic origin, became a nationally protected geographical indication product. In 2014, the China Light Industry Federation and the China Household Products Industry Association jointly awarded the title of "Incense Capital of China" to Dapu Town, Yongchun County, Fujian Province.

Incense is of great use. German writer Süskind once said in his masterpiece, *Perfume*: He who ruled scent ruled the hearts of men. In an era when a host of internationally renowned brands are carefully concocting scents, the oriental scent from Yongchun, an ancient luxury, has always been there.

May this scent fill the whole world.

传承至今的蒲庆兰香室。（刘宝生 摄）
The time-honored Pu Qinglan Incense Store. (Photo by Liu Baosheng)

传统体育与医药：
铁拳争道义，妙手捧仁心

Traditional Physical Exercises and Medicine

五祖拳：宋太祖一脉拳法，开五叶远播五洲

Wuzuquan (Five Ancestor Fist Kung Fu), a Southern Shaolin Chinese Martial Art

泉州刣狮：练拳头保自己，练刣狮保乡里

Quanzhou Zhongshi (Shaolin Lion Dance)

灵源万应茶：护身健体菩提丸，海外游子称万应

Lingyuan Wanying Tea (Lingyuan Medicinal Tea)

五祖拳：
宋太祖一脉拳法，开五叶远播五洲

膜拜武术者，都对五祖拳心向往之。

它本是一套帝王拳，由宋太祖赵匡胤所创的北派太祖拳法“三十二式太祖长拳”经历史演变进化而来，发轫于宋，成熟于明，至清初臻于完备。宋建炎年间，南外宗正司迁泉州，三千余赵氏皇族成员于此定居，太祖拳亦随之融入当地。明清以来，泉州人以太祖拳为本体，发展出一门五拳的拳法体系，即所谓“一达尊，二太祖，三罗汉，四行者，五白鹤”，五拳种分布于闽南各地，套路两百有余，且各具特点。其中以人命拳者，是硬功直进的太祖拳和注重内养的达尊拳；因形取象者，则为气势威武的罗汉拳、灵活敏捷的行者拳以及动静有法的白鹤拳。五祖拳技手简约，拳势激烈，劲力刚猛又刚柔相济，极富实战性。其一门五拳，拳风相似，功理相通，技手相仿，步马相同，既可兼习，亦可专精，入门后易于举一反三，各式拳家名手辈出，同出一宗又各树一帜，造就五祖拳多地区、多流派、多风格的历史风貌。

五祖拳师傅在泉州古厝里传授拳法。（陈英杰 摄）
A master of Wuzuquan is teaching in a traditional residence of Quanzhou. (Photo by Chen Yingjie)

Wuzuquan (Five-Ancestor Fist Kung Fu), a Southern Shaolin Chinese Martial Art

Those who are fascinated by Chinese martial arts will surely be attracted by Wuzuquan.

Originating in the Song Dynasty, maturing in the Ming Dynasty and reaching perfection in the early Qing Dynasty, Wuzuquan was originally a bare-handed martial art form with thirty-two postures called Taizu Chang Quan (Taizu Long Fist) out of respect for its creator Zhao Kuangyin, founder of the Song Dynasty. Taizu Long Fist was introduced to Quanzhou by the three thousand or more imperial clan members who moved here during the Southern Song Dynasty. Since the Ming and Qing dynasties, the people of Quanzhou have developed a system of five styles of fist forms based on Taizu Long Fist, namely Bodhidharma Fist (Dazun Quan), Great Ancestor Fist (Taizu Quan), Arhat Fist (Luohan Quan), Monkey Fist (Hou Quan) and White Crane Fist (Baihe Quan), hence the name "Five-Ancestor". With more than 200 routines featuring different characteristics, the five styles are distributed throughout Southern Fujian. Among them, the Great Ancestor Fist features the precision and efficient movements, Bodhidharma Fist the breathing methods, Arhat Fist the posture and dynamic power of Arhat, Monkey Fist the nimbleness and agility, and White Crane Fist the complementary softness and hardness. Of one origin, the five kinds of fist are similar in style, theory, techniques and footwork, so they can be practised either concurrently or separately. And it is easy to draw inferences from one another after getting started. However, the five styles of fists which are popular in different regions, possess their distinctive characteristics and each style boasts its own famous martial artists.

“拳头、烧酒、曲”，尚武的泉州人对于五祖拳的天然偏好自不待言。这种情愫实则可以看作追慕南少林武术文化的一个缩影。君不见，历朝泉州名臣显宦多知兵而好武，宋代名相曾公亮编撰的《武经总要》和明代抗倭名将俞大猷编撰的《续武经总要》是中国历史上两部重要的军事著作，后者的《剑经》是中国第一部武术专著。其后，俞大猷更是将少林棍法回传给嵩山少林寺，被称为“少林俞家棍”，收于《少林武术大全》，成为武林一段佳话。

罡风振正的泉州武林一度名将辈出，俞大猷、郑成功、施琅、林兴珠、陈化成等一大批英杰至今仍为人民所追怀。他们始终践行“武之大者，为国为民”的精神，从抗倭到复台，从抵御外侮到保家卫国，无不显示其侠肝义胆。

随着海上丝绸之路的延伸和华侨出洋的足迹，五祖拳也远播五大洲，享誉全世界。人们更是将南少林文化与南音、南戏、南建筑、南派工艺并称为泉州“五南”。

我武惟扬，蹈厉奋发。武林从未逝去，今天的刺桐城仍在赓续华夏武术文明的精神，内外兼修的泉州人常常演绎文魁武侠之经典故事。

张弛之间，从容于山海，是真功夫，乃成旷世传奇。

泉州市中小学生南少林五祖拳健身操会操比赛。（陈晓东 摄）
A competition of Southern Shaolin Wuzuquan for primary and secondary school students in Quanzhou. (Photo by Chen Xiaodong)

Southern Shaolin Martial Arts, wine and Nanyin Music, with these three parts inseparable in their lives, people of Quanzhou, undoubtedly have a special preference for Wuzuquan, which epitomizes how enthusiastic the admiration of Southern Shaolin Martial Arts is here. In ancient China, most of the high-ranking officials from Quanzhou were both military strategists and kung fu masters. *The Complete Essentials for the Military Classics* compiled by the famous prime minister Zeng Gongliang in about 1043 and *A Continuation of the Complete Essentials for the Military Classics* co-written by Yu Dayou in 1557 were two of the most important military works in Chinese history. Yu's another work, *A Treatise on the Sword*, was the first monograph on martial arts in China. A far-spread story at the time was about the exchange of kung fu skills between Yu and Shaolin Temple. Around 1560, Yu Dayou traveled to Shaolin Temple to observe the Shaolin monks' fighting techniques. As a reward, he returned to the south along with two monks, Zongqing and Pucong. Over the next three years, he taught them the "Yu Family Staff", a set of staff movement techniques he created.

In the world of Quanzhou martial arts, there were once a great number of heroic figures, such as Yu Dayou, Zheng Chenggong, Shi Lang, Lin Xingzhu and Chen Huacheng, who are still alive in the memory of people. Be it the fight against Japanese pirates or the recovery of Taiwan, or the resistance against foreign invasion, they always lived up to the spirit of great martial artists who served their country and their people with their kung fu.

With the extension of the Maritime Silk Road, the footprints of the Chinese covered the whole world and Wuzuquan was spread and won worldwide popularity. Today, Southern Shaolin Martial Arts, Nanyin Music, southern operas, southern architecture and southern craftsmanship are referred to as the "Five Souths" (five unique cultures) of Quanzhou.

Traditional martial arts like Wuzuquan have been passed down from generation to generation in Quanzhou and the spirit of martial arts has inspired people here to aim high and work hard.

Nourished by this very spirit, the industrious and daring people of Quanzhou have created one miracle after another to live up to their belief: Winners never quit and quitters never win.

泉州刣狮：
练拳头保自己，练刣狮保乡里

它是中华阵法武术的活化石，脱胎于少林武学，保留了十几种珍贵的古代阵法；它是团队精神的教科书，拒绝一腔孤勇，讲究共同进退的整体艺术。在和平年代，它把相互依存、众志成城的尚武之风生动地演绎成酬神祈福的地方风俗。

提及刣狮，泉州人无不竖起大拇指，那股自豪感仿佛在向世人昭示：这就是咱厝的守护之阵。

泉州刣狮相传为少林和尚一元祖师创建，是流行于闽南地区的一项武术活动。闽南话里“刣”意为“斗杀”，即“斗杀狮子”。表演时，由两人扮成狮子，其狮头、狮口、狮眼、狮尾、狮皮都可以动，其他人扮成武士，手持刀枪剑戟和盾牌等十八般武器，包围着狮子“大打出手”，那场面麇集了刀光剑影，表演者不时发出阵阵吼声，令人惊心动魄。

如果有幸见识此阵，你会发现，刣狮队的表演形式十分丰富，几乎每种兵器都有多种套路，可以按照不同的出击对象摆出不同的阵法，阵容则有几人、十几人、几十人等等。其中最为出众的是宋江阵，此阵最早出现于明末清初，俗称“套宋江”。

最为有趣的是，刣狮在表演中有一番精彩搏杀的设计，寓攻防于表演中，形成独特的武术美学。所谓“青狮白目眉，要刣任你来”（泉州本地话，意思是如果出阵表演的狮子道具颜色是青色，狮头的眉毛画的是白色，那么谁都可以来比试），要求表演者十八般武艺精通，刣狮队伍从套路的演练到招法使用，需要较长时间的严格训练，表演时要求快、准、狠，真实生动。

威武的白眉青狮。（陈小阳 摄）
The mighty white-browed green lion. (Photo by Chen Xiaoyang)

Quanzhou Zhongshi (Shaolin Lion Dance)

Born out of Shaolin martial arts, Quanzhou Zhongshi, a kind of lion dance, preserves a dozen or more rare ancient formations. It is a living fossil of tactical formations in Chinese martial arts as well as a textbook of team spirit, refusing being alone and focusing on the whole art of advancing and retreating together. In times of peace, it vividly translates the interdependence and unity of strength into a local custom of rewarding the gods and praying for good fortune.

When it comes to Zhongshi, the people of Quanzhou will all give a thumbs-up and be overtaken by a sense of pride for this is their guardian formation.

Quanzhou Zhongshi is said to have been created by a Shaolin monk, Master Yiyuan, and is a popular martial art performance in Southern Fujian. In Minnan dialect "zhong" actually means lionfighting, namely, the fight against lions. During the performance, two dancers operate the lion costume, of which the head, the mouth, the eyes, the tail and the skin can be moved, while others who are dressed as warriors armed with the typical weapons of traditional Chinese martial arts such as axes, spears, swords, forks and shields, surround the lion in a big fight. It's a thrilling spectacle flashing with knives and swords, with roars from time to time.

If you are lucky enough to watch Zhongshi, you'll find that it includes a great variety of performances, in which the eighteen Shaolin weapons, each with multiple routines, can be arrayed in different formations according to the target of attack. The number of people involved in a formation varies from a few, a dozen to several dozens. The most spectacular one is a spellbinding formation named Song Jiang Zhen (Song Jiang Battle Array) that first appeared during the late Ming and early Qing dynasties, in which the story of Song Jiang, a Chinese literary historical figure who led an armed rebellion against the ruling Song Dynasty in the early 12th century, was performed.

The most interesting part of Quanzhou Zhongshi lies in the fighting against the lion in which martial art attack and defense are integrated. A tradition in Quanzhou says that if the lion is green with white eyebrows, any other troupes are welcome to challenge and fight it out. As the performances need to be fast, accurate, resolute and vivid, the performers are required to be proficient in all eighteen Shaolin weapons, and it takes a long time to train a lion dance troupe in terms of routines and techniques.

泉州刣狮的核心要素是古代战场拼杀的真艺功夫，源于明代泉州抗倭民族英雄俞大猷以太祖拳棒和兵战阵法训练军民抗击倭寇，其时采用的兵战阵法和武艺训练成为独一无二的阵法武术。

阵法武术在明末清初融入杀狮技击，《西山杂志》记载：“南邑朴里、水头之技击青狮白眉……石狮、深沪、祥芝……诸村杀狮技击，俱聘吾族之传授焉。”在反清复明的斗争中，天地会以“杀青狮”暗喻“杀清师”，刣狮成为狮阵武术，流传至今。

岁月更迭，一代代狮阵团队在传承的过程中，不断铸就闽南人爱国爱家、爱拼敢赢的集体性格特质，随着时代发展，这种家国情怀转化为建设家乡、热心公益的精神动力。

昨日种种，是骁猛与膂力，捍卫了一方水土的完整；今朝幕幕，是庇佑与祈攘，濡养着一片家园的繁息。化剑为犁，偃武修文，爱与和平才是新时代的阵法向心力。

狮阵表演。（陈晓东 摄）
A performance of the lion dance. (Photo by Chen Xiaodong)

The core elements of Quanzhou Zhongshi are the fighting techniques from ancient battlefields, which originated in the Ming Dynasty when Yu Dayou, a national hero resisting Japanese invasion trained his soldiers and people to fight against Japanese pirates with the unique combination of the martial art, Wuzuquan and military tactics.

During the late Ming and early Qing dynasties, in the struggle against the Qing Dynasty to restore the Ming Dynasty, Tiandi Hui (the Heaven and Earth Association or the Triads) integrated the performance techniques of fighting and killing of green lions with white eyebrows with tactical formations as a metaphor for "killing the Qing division" because of their similar pronunciation. Records of this can be found in *Xishan Miscellaneous Records* by Cai Yongjian, a Qing Dynasty scholar from Quanzhou: "The techniques of the fighting and killing of green lions with white eyebrows performed in Puli and Shuitou of Nan'an are taught by Master Liaofan, a warrior monk from the Southern Shaolin Temple and the performance was spread to places such as Shishi, Shenhu and Xiangzhi."

Over the years, by working together constructively to create a seamless performance, generations of lion dance teams have fostered a spirit of patriotism, teamwork and optimism, which, with the progress of the times, has been transformed into a spiritual drive to devote to the building of their hometown and to make earnest efforts to promote the public good.

Zhongshi used to help safeguard the territorial integrity of China, but now, in the peacetime of ours, it has become a custom where people could pray for good luck, safety and happiness.

灵源万应茶：
护身健体菩提丸，海外游子称万应

山曰灵源，海拔三百米，二十四峰簇拥，峰峰相挽，层峦叠翠，药用植被十分丰富；水唤晋江，逶迤数百里，泽被两岸，咆哮东行，滋养所行之处。

一味药茶，浑似投胎这山水中的精灵，只因圣手采撷，方得长生奇效，六百三十载春秋轮回，口碑相传，普济众生。

在闽南，人们亲切地称其为“灵源万应茶”，民间有“家有万应茶，安心一整夏”的说法。灵源万应茶始创于明，其创制人为明代灵源寺三十一世祖沐讲禅师。据《泉郡晋南地名探源·寺庵考附录》（卷十六之三）灵源寺历代僧尼名录记载：“明三十一世祖沐讲，俗姓张名定边，陈友谅部将。元末友谅举事兵败，张于洪武元年戊申遁入泉南灵源山隐居，为避前嫌削发为僧，自号沐讲禅师。入空门后，不闻尘俗事，究心佛理，率住山旧僧尼志尚、利济取山中之百草，用姑师井之水泡制药饼，广施万民，不求图报。”

名茶出于名寺，灵源寺是泉南一带香火极盛的琅嬛福地，相传早在隋初，就有僧人于灵源山顶立寺，祀奉观音大士。它远离红尘闹市，静卧山间，规模宏大，气势非凡，又因沐讲禅师的大德，更显寺名。

阳光下的灵源寺建筑群。（施清凉 摄）
The Lingyuan Temple complex in the sunshine. (Photo by Shi Qingliang)

Lingyuan Wanying Tea (Lingyuan Medicinal Tea)

There in Jinjiang, a satellite city of Quanzhou, is a mountain called Lingyuan Mountain which is 300 meters above sea level. The mountain, surrounded by twenty-four overlapping peaks, is green and rich in medical vegetation. Winding for hundreds of miles through the city, is a river called Jinjiang River which roars eastwards nourishing the areas it travels.

Bred in this place of greatness and beauty is a household medicinal tea called Wanying (giving response to every prayer) Tea, which boasts a history of some 630 years.

A long-held nickname for the tea in Southern Fujian is Panacea Tea, for people here believe that a pack of it in hand guarantees them a healthy summer. Lingyuan Wanying Tea was first created in the Ming Dynasty by the 31st generation ancestor of Lingyuan Temple, Master Mujiang. According to the directory of monks and nuns of the past generations in *The Origin of Place Names in Jinjiang and Nan'an, Quanzhou Prefecture, Appendix to the Investigation of Temples and Nunneries* (Vol. 16 No. 3), the 31st generation ancestor of Lingyuan Temple, Master Mujiang, secular name Zhang Dingbian, was a general in the army of Chen Youliang who was the founder and first emperor of Chen Han, a short-lived state in the late Yuan Dynasty and early Ming Dynasty. When Chen was defeated, Zhang retreated to Lingyuan Mountain in Quanzhou in 1368, and to avoid the former enemies, he shaved his hair to become a monk and named himself Master Mujiang. Thereafter, he completely withdrew from the worldly affairs and devoted himself to the study of Buddhism. He led a monk named Zhishang and a nun named Liji to gather a great variety of herbs from the mountain and used the water from Gushi Well to make free medicines for people.

The famous tea comes from the famous temple and Lingyuan Temple is a blessed place in the south of Quanzhou which attracts endless worshipers. Far away from the bustling city and lying quietly in the mountains, the magnificent and grand temple is said to have been built by a monk on top of Lingyuan Mountain to worship Guanyin, the God of Mercy, and later shot to fame after Master Mujiang's producing and distributing free medicines to people

沐讲禅师每遇山气绝佳时节，总会踏遍青山，遍寻制作药茶的材料。他悉心采集山茶、鬼针、青蒿、飞扬草、爵床、野甘草、墨旱莲等十七种青草药，加入上等茶叶，再配以其他中药，精心炮制，所得精华定名为“菩提丸”，供患病僧尼煎服及善男信女取用。

六百多年来，寺中僧尼世世代代传承此秘方，悉心保护。菩提丸历经演绎、传承、发展，到 1951 年，灵源寺僧王广武将菩提丸改制成灵源万应茶，该茶具有疏风解表、调胃健脾、祛痰利湿之功能，对伤风感冒发热、中暑痢疾、腹痛吐泻等疾病疗效显著，更是一种防暑降温的理想药茶。

随着时代进步，如今的灵源万应茶既承袭传统的制作技艺，也辅以现代化的制药设备、净化车间和检测技术，演绎六百年历史、历经六百年传承、实现六百年发展。在泉州、港澳台等地以及东南亚一些区域，在海外闽籍华人中间，灵源万应茶可谓无人不知、无人不晓。

中国人以茶代药、防病祛病的养生传统，早在上古神农氏时期就已开启，并成为中华文化的重要组成部分。灵源万应茶秉承茶道文化的精髓，成就了一代药茶专家，在闽南地区，特别是沿海一带，是广大人民群众在生产生活中预防疾病、增进健康不可或缺的必备良药。

茶非茶，非常茶；药非药，非常药。百草源为灵，功成万应生！

晋江万应茶文化园里的沐讲禅师雕像。（施清凉 摄）
A statue of Master Mujiang in the Wanying Tea Culture Park in Jinjiang. (Photo by Shi Qingliang)

When the weather was perfect, Master Mujiang would trek up the green hills in search of ingredients to make medicinal tea. He collected seventeen herbs, including wild tea leaves, beggarticks, Artemisia apiacea, Euphorbia hirta, creeping rostellularia herb and eclipta, added in fine tea leaves and other Chinese herbs, combined and processed them into a medical essence that formed into pills named "Bodhi Pills", which he offered to sick monks, nuns, followers and believers.

For more than 600 years, generations of monks and nuns from the temple have carefully protected the secret recipe, polished it and passed it on. And in 1951, Wang Guangwu, a monk of Lingyuan Temple, changed the Bodhi Pills into Lingyuan Wanying Tea, which has the functions of dispelling wind, relieving exterior syndrome, regulating stomach and strengthening spleen, eliminating phlegm and promoting diuresis. The tea, best known to have been an ideal medicinal tea for heatstroke prevention, also has remarkable curative effects on cold, fever, heatstroke, dysentery, abdominal pain and vomiting.

With the passage of time, Lingyuan Wanying Tea incorporates modern pharmaceutical equipment, purification workshops and quality control measures into its processing while inheriting the 600-year traditional producing techniques, making it a household name in Quanzhou, Hongkong, Macao, Taiwan and some Southeast Asian regions as well as places where overseas Chinese from Southern Fujian live.

The Chinese health-preserving tradition of substituting tea for medicine to prevent and cure diseases traces its history to a time before written records began at the era of the Divine Farmer, Shennong, the legendary inventor of agriculture and medicine as well as the finder of tea, and has always been an important part of Chinese culture. Inheriting the essence of tea culture, Lingyuan Wanying Tea has become a highly effective medicinal tea. In Southern Fujian, especially in coastal areas, it is a household necessity helping people to prevent diseases and improve their health in their daily life.

Different from ordinary tea and different from prescribed drug liquid as well, Wanying Tea, as the name suggests, is a miracle tea with medicinal effects.

传统民俗：诸神大派对，逗阵嘉年华

Traditional Folk Customs

泉州闹元宵习俗：
满城如昼上元夜，一国若狂看妆人

“每个不曾起舞的日子，都是对生命的一种辜负。”1896年，近代哲学大师尼采借超人之口，在《查拉图斯特拉如是说》中发出呼号。尼采无缘见识中国的狂欢节，更无从想象泉州人在闹元宵的节日氛围里挣脱日常理性禁锢的种种图景。但这或许不是他一个人的遗憾，而是未曾邂逅此节日的人们集体的遗憾。

泉州闹元宵有灯会、灯猜、妆人、唱戏、乞龟等内容，著名应节食品有元宵圆、润饼菜。很多家庭还在元宵日祭祀祖先、追思祖德。

泉州闹元宵的重头戏还属灯会。武则天久视元年（700），泉州开始建城，其时就有上元花灯活动。唐僖宗广明元年（880），河南固始人傅实以威武军节度招讨使从长安带兵入闽，镇守泉州，聘紫云黄守恭五世孙女为夫人。隔年元宵节前，黄家送红、白莲花灯一对，预祝早生贵子，从此开泉南上元娘家送灯先河。后傅实移居南安丰州桃源，建唐王宫，元宵按照长安结灯仪式与民同乐，往后相沿成俗。“天下上元，灯烛之盛，无逾闽中”是古时泉州闹花灯盛况的真实记载。

人头攒动的泉州元宵节。（视觉中国 供图）
The crowded Lantern Festival in Quanzhou. (Courtesy of VCG.COM)

The Lantern Festival Traditions of Quanzhou

"And let each day be a loss to us on which we did not dance once!" Friedrich Nietzsche, the modern philosopher, thus exclaimed through the Superman in his book *Thus Spoke Zarathustra: A Book for All and None* in 1896. Nietzsche had no chance of seeing the Chinese carnival for himself, let alone imagining the pictures of how people of Quanzhou break free from their daily routines and enjoy the Lantern Festival. This, however, may not be his own regret but the regret of those who have never been able to chance upon this festival.

In Quanzhou, activities for the Lantern Festival include watching lantern shows, guessing lantern riddles, lantern parades, opera singing, Qigui ceremony (praying to the turtle for luck and safety), etc. And famous festival foods include Yuanxiao (sweet sticky rice balls) and spring rolls. Many families also worship their ancestors on the Lantern Festival.

However, the highlight of the festival is the lantern show. In 700, when Quanzhou was first built as a city, there were activities during the Lantern Festival. Then in 880, Fu Shi, a native of Gushi in Henan Province brought troops from Chang'an (today's Xi'an) to Fujian as the military governor and he later married the great-great-great granddaughter of Huang Shougong, the once richest man in Quanzhou. The next year, before the Lantern Festival, the Huang family sent the daughter a pair of red and white lotus lanterns to wish for an early birth of a son, because in the Southern Fujian dialect, the pronunciation of "lantern" is similar to that of "son". Thereafter, the tradition of sending a pair of lanterns to the newlywed daughters during the Lantern Festival started in Quanzhou. Fu later moved to live in Taoyuan, Fengzhou in Nan'an, the satellite city of Quanzhou, and built the Palace of Tang Emperor to honor Emperor Taizong of the Tang Dynasty. During the Lantern Festival, he followed the tradition of Chang'an, organized activities and celebrated the festival with local folks and thereby passed it down as a tradition. And the grand and festive atmosphere of the Lantern Festival in Quanzhou was vividly depicted in some historical records.

“有灯无月不娱人，有月无灯不算春。”泉州灯会习俗包括挂灯、送灯、观灯（赏灯）、点灯、游灯等，古时还有抢灯。作为集体的文化盛宴，此夜家家户户挂花灯，男女老少成群结队上街赏灯，黄发垂髫，怡然自乐。如有新嫁女儿的人家，要给亲家送红、白莲花灯和观音送子灯。孩童们手提春灯，点上灯火，走街串巷嬉戏“游灯”。若点灯时不慎把灯烧了，叫作“出灯”，因泉州方言里“灯”与“丁”同音，“出灯”就是“出丁”，寓意人丁兴旺。

泉州元宵踩街古称“妆人”，此习俗在中原几乎绝迹。明代《闽书》载：“泉中上元后数日，大赛神像，装扮故事，盛饰珠宝，钟鼓震轰，一国若狂。”踩街时会表演阵头、花灯、彩车、南少林武术及各种游艺，如果有人放鞭炮，队伍要暂停表演表示感谢。

每年春节前，泉州、澎湖两地天后宫还会联合举行“乞龟”祈福活动，两地的制龟师傅聚在一起，共同制作米龟，并在元宵节当天举行米龟点睛仪式，寓意来年幸福安康。

随着海丝路上不断扬帆，闹元宵的传统文化在五洲四海的闽南文化圈开枝散叶，形成深远的民俗记忆和广泛的族群共鸣。

“还似旧时游上苑，车如流水马如龙。花月正春风。”新时代赓续老传统，吹散乡愁多少恨，为欢此夜月明中。

2024年2月22日，泉州霞洲妈祖宫与台湾澎湖天后宫联合举办米龟点睛祈福仪式。（中新图片 供图）
Eye-Dotting Ceremony for the Rice Turtle, a blessing ceremony praying for family harmony and cross-Strait peace, was jointly held by Tianhou (Mazu) Temple of Penghu County in Taiwan and Mazu Temple of Xiazhou Community in Quanzhou on February 22, 2024. (Courtesy of CNSphoto.com)

On the night of the Lantern Festival, if there's no moon but brilliant lanterns, one won't enjoy himself to the full, while if there are no lanterns but only the moon, it doesn't make a spring. The Lantern Festival is a local carnival. The customs of Quanzhou Lantern Festival include hanging lanterns, gifting lanterns, appreciating lanterns, lighting lanterns and parading lanterns, and in ancient times, there was even a tradition of lantern snatching. It's a time of great happiness and every family hangs lanterns on this night. Men and women, young and old go out in groups to enjoy the lanterns in the streets. If a family has a newly-married daughter, they must give her a pair of red and white lotus lanterns together with a lantern of Guanyin (the God of Mercy) carrying a child. Children carry their lanterns, light them and go from street to street. If a lantern is accidentally burned when lightened, it is an auspicious sign, suggesting that the family will grow.

The custom of Lantern Festival parade was introduced, in ancient times, to Quanzhou from the Central Plains, where it is almost extinct today. In *The Book of Min*, a book on Fujian Province written during the Ming Dynasty, the Lantern Festival of Quanzhou is depicted as a local carnival during which a great many people, beaming with joy and accompanied by loud and lively music, dressed up as different characters and joined the parade on the streets, which included various music and acrobatic performances, exhibition of lanterns and floats as well as performances of Southern Shaolin martial arts. And if someone set off firecrackers, the team would stop performing for a while to express their gratitude.

Every year, before the Spring Festival, Tianhou temples (The Palace of Goddess Mazu) in Quanzhou and Penghu will jointly hold a prayer event, Qigui Ceremony, during which turtle makers from both places get together to make a giant rice turtle with bags of rice and hold an eye-dotting ceremony on the day of the Lantern Festival, offering prayers for happiness and well-being in the coming year.

With the revitalization of the Maritime Silk Road, the traditional culture of celebrating the Lantern Festival has been spread all over the world to where people of Southern Fujian origin live and forming a strong cultural bond as well as a profound culture memory and widespread community resonance.

Every Lantern Festival, festive atmosphere is in the air when celebrations that have been handed down for generations begin, in real life and in the memory of those who are far away from home.

闽台东石灯俗：
正月十三祭三公，跨越海峡来卜灯

同名不同城，共数一宫灯。

在海峡两岸，有这样一种特殊的现象，福建众多城镇村落的地名，在台湾常能悉数对应找到。同根同源、不忘祖庭的拳拳乡情，在此淋漓尽致地生发。由此，更演绎出无数感人的“双城记”。

福建晋江市东石镇与台湾嘉义县布袋镇东石乡，就是这样一对双子星。它们分别坐落于两岸滨海地区，共同拥抱着一个全国独一无二的元宵灯俗。其独特之处在于：只在这两地之间流传。

它的上演时间并非正月十五，而是自每年正月十三始，为期三天之长。依惯例，闽台两东石上一年新结婚的新郎官，都必须于正月十三前把新娘陪嫁的宫灯挂到晋江东石母乡三公宫里，三公宫内除各新婚夫妻送来的宫灯外，正中还有一盏由公家定制的大红绣球灯。

热闹温馨的卜灯仪式现场。（视觉中国 供图）
The lively and warm scene of Dongshi Lantern Festival custom, Budeng (prediction of the number of children one may have). (Courtesy of VCG.COM)

Dongshi Lantern Festival Custom of Fujian and Taiwan

They are different cities with the same name and share the same Lantern Festival custom.

The Fujian-Taiwan region has been a cultural one with the same root and common source since ancient times, so it feels special but not surprising to find that the names of many towns and villages of Fujian can often be found in Taiwan. This is probably the best testimony of Taiwan residents' nostalgic feeling and sentimental attachment to their ancestral homes in the mainland of China and thereby contributes to countless touching "tales of two cities".

Dongshi Town in Jinjiang City, Fujian Province and Dongshi Village in Budai Town, Jiayi County, Taiwan Province are twin towns as such. Located in the coastal area on both sides across the Taiwan Strait, the two places embrace a Lantern Festival custom that is unique in China. And the uniqueness lies in that the custom is jointly celebrated only by people of these two places.

Instead of taking place on the 15th of the first lunar month, the celebrations start on the 13th and last for three whole days. It is customary for the grooms of the newlyweds in the counterparts of Fujian and Taiwan to hang palace lanterns in Jiaying Temple (also Sangong Temple, Temple of the Three Lords of the Nine Dragons) in Jinjiang Dongshi. These lanterns are part of the dowries of their brides wishing for the early birth of a son, as "lantern" and "son" have the same pronunciation in the Southern Fujian dialect. And besides the lanterns sent by the newlyweds, there is a large red silk embroidered lantern custom-made by the organization in the middle of the temple.

活动的最高潮在元宵夜的午夜时分到来。两地代表须齐聚三公宫，毕恭毕敬地聆听主事者通报今年台湾及本地的宫灯数。待共庆两岸人丁兴旺后，即开启灯俗的重头戏——卜灯之旅。所谓“卜灯”，即新郎官们在三公爷座前掷筊杯，掷得杯数最多的人大放鞭炮，用大红甲吹把大红绣球灯迎回家。随后，其他人也将各自的宫灯迎回家，挂在新房内，祈求三公爷保佑婚姻幸福美满，早生贵子。

台湾乡亲代表参与卜灯时，若掷得大红绣球灯，十六日得专船送回台湾，本地则必须出动蜈蚣阁隆重欢送。

闽台东石元宵灯俗见证了两岸民俗相同、神缘相通、血脉相连的牵绊。历史上晋江东石人跨海播迁，筚路蓝缕，始成今日声势浩大的延绵根系。两岸共数宫灯、传灯的足迹即树高千尺不忘根的心迹。

“棠棣之华，鄂不韡韡。凡今之人，莫如兄弟。”吹落了思乡的尘，却吹不去额头的纹；走完了天下的路，才想起了回家的门。风吹年华的梦，落叶总要归根。

两岸宗亲在三公宫里一起数宫灯。（陈起拓 摄）
Clansmen from both sides of the Taiwan Strait are counting the number of lanterns together at Jiaying Temple. (Photo by Chen Qituo)

The climax of the event comes at midnight on the night of the Lantern Festival. Bridegrooms from both Taiwan and Jinjiang gather at Jiaying Temple to listen respectfully to the ceremonial master's announcement of the number of lanterns in the two places this year. After celebrating the prosperity in population of both sides across the Taiwan Strait comes the high light of the custom, Budeng (prediction of the number of children one may have). The bridegrooms are invited to the front of the Three Lords worshiped in the temple to toss a pair of half-moon shaped bamboo plaques for divination. The one who outnumbers all the others will set off firecrackers and welcome the large red silk embroidered lantern home with a band of woodwind and percussion instruments whilst the players wearing long red silk scarves. Afterwards, other bridegrooms also take their own lanterns home and hang them in the bridal chamber to pray for the blessing of the Three Lords for a happy and prosperous marriage and the early birth of a child.

If it is a Taiwan bridegroom who wins the large red silk embroidered lantern, he'll be sent back to Taiwan on a special boat on the 16th and the local community will have to give him a send-off with Wugongge, or Taige, a parade and folk dance originating in Southern Song Dynasty which is performed with teenagers dressed up as characters from historical stories or legends standing high on plank platforms and other people carrying poles below parading on the streets.

The Lantern Festival custom shared in two places both named Dongshi from Fujian and Taiwan is a testimony to the ties that bind the two sides across the Taiwan Strait with the same folk culture, religious belief and blood. Throughout history, many people from Dongshi, Jinjiang have migrated in search of work, spreading their influence across the world and leaving behind a legacy of shared culture and traditions. The shared Lantern Festival custom is a perfect illustration of the old saying, a tree though a thousand feet tall, never forgets its roots.

The bond between brothers is like that of flowers on the same branch, or hands and feet. Only brothers will share weal and woe; only brothers will help each other in times of trouble. "Young, I left home and not till old do I come back. Unchanged is my accent, yet my hair no longer black." However far one may travel, he'll never forget to go back home.

南安英都拔拔灯习俗：海丝内河拉纤夫，昭惠庙前拔拔灯

正月初九，闽南唤作“天公生”，天公即玉帝。面对掌管天庭上界的一把手，无人敢不虔诚祀奉。这一天的闽南人自然是分外忙碌的，但泉州南安英都人似乎更忙。因为除了供天、敬神之外，他们还有一个特殊的节目马上开锣——英都拔拔灯。

南安英都拔拔灯习俗源于古代英溪的纤夫拉纤劳作。英都镇位于南安西部，英溪贯穿全境，注入晋江西溪，是历史上海上丝绸之路东端的内河驿渡之一。英溪滩险弯多，为祈求顺风顺水，船夫们从九日山昭惠庙请来海神仁福王分灵立庙，也叫昭惠庙，俗称董山宫。相传“有董山宫，就有拔拔灯”。一年一度，万里归乡，拔拔灯是恳亲联谊桥梁，也是闽南人聚族而居、注重亲情的文化表征。

当日晌午，英都洪氏后人以各宗支房份为单位，着手准备灯阵。只见每阵均将粗大绳索紧缚于柱子或树干之间，那绳上悬挂着固定的灯笼，约五十厘米间隔一盏。灯阵长短视该房份人丁多少而定。

傍晚时分，各房份的灯阵便浩浩荡荡地从自家出发，到昭惠庙前会合。此时，每阵须选一壮硕青年领头，胸前缚一扁担，肩负大绳，以船夫拉纤姿势弓身下沉，拉动灯阵向前行进，其状神似拔船拉纤。

灯阵出发。（彭燕珍 / 张九强 摄）
Departure of the lantern team. (Photo by Peng Yanzhen and Zhang Jiuqiang)

Baba Deng Lantern Parade in Yingdu, Nan'an

The 9th day of the first lunar month is important for people in Southern Fujian, because it's the birthday of Tiangong, the Jade Emperor. While everyone are busy paying homage to the supreme deity of Chinese tradition, residents of Yingdu Town in Nan'an, one of the satellite cities of Quanzhou, are even busier. Apart from offering sacrifices to heaven and worshiping God, they also hold a special event—Yingdu Baba Deng Lantern Parade.

The custom of Baba Deng in Yingdu Town originated from the barge haulers who worked along Yingxi Creek in ancient times. Yingdu Town lies in the west of Nan'an with Yingxi running through the whole territory and pouring into Xixi Creek, a tributary of Jinjiang River. Yingxi is one of the inland river ferries at the east end of the ancient Maritime Silk Road. There are many dangerous bends along Yingxi Creek. In order to pray for a smooth sailing, the boatmen invited the Sea God, King Renfu, from Zhaohui Temple in Jiuri Mountain to Yingdu, and set up a branch Zhaohui Temple, commonly known as Dongshangong Temple. It is said that where there is a Dongshangong Temple, there is the Baba Deng Lantern Parade. Held once a year, the lantern parade is a bridge of friendship as well as a manifestation of the clan-based living culture in Southern Fujian which lays special emphasis on family ties.

At noon that day, members of the Hong clan in Yingdu are divided into different teams in accordance with their branches and set about preparing for the lantern formations. For each team, a thick rope is tied to two pillars or tree trunks, on which lanterns are hung at intervals of about 50 cm. And the length of a team depends on the size of the branch.

In the evening, the lantern teams of each branch set off from their own houses to meet in front of Zhaohui Temple. At this time, each team must choose a strong young man as their leader. With a shoulder pole tied to his chest and a huge rope on his shoulder, the young man leans forward and pulls the rope of lanterns forward the way a barge hauler pulled a boat in the old days.

待得会灯礼成，众人抬出神轿，迎仁福王起驾出宫。至此，拔拔灯队伍才算正式出动。护驾灯阵的出场顺序大有讲究，须得由灯首在庙里抽签决定。威风凛凛的仁福王神轿由灯首扛抬，稳列灯阵队伍中间。前有四支火把探路，呼应着大锣、大吹、大刀、大旗开道，后有一个灯阵专门护驾，伴以伞、扇等执事及一队英都大鼓吹。

各路灯阵次第有序，整个阵仗如长蛇一般，须先沿庙前名唤“五斗”的大片田地环行三圈，仿效金蛇蜕壳之动作，寄寓新岁开启，春雷乍响，万物复苏。

此般隆重的仪式之后，灯阵才可向洪氏家庙挺进谒祖，并绕洪氏家庙巡游庆祝。此后，各房份灯阵返回本自然村，着手迎接全境大巡游。游行队伍所到之处，各家各户都在门前燃烧篝火、放鞭炮，称为“迎灯”。值任灯首之家，有一项特殊权利——请仁福王的神轿停下来，上供烧香许愿，称为“留灯”。“迎灯”“留灯”即迎丁、留丁，寓意增添人丁。

巡游全境礼毕，众灯阵散去，只留一队灯阵为仁福王护驾回銮。待仁福王回銮入庙后，灯首上香祷告，当年的使命才告完成。然后，由有威望的长者在庙中掷杯，决定新一轮灯首。至此，一年一度的拔拔灯仪式圆满结束。

英都拔拔灯再现了当年英溪纤夫拉纤行船的场景，从一个特殊角度反映出泉州海上丝绸之路内河驿渡运输的繁荣状况。其所拔出的阵势和力量，昭示这里的人们可以向生活弯腰，却从不对苦难低头。一步一个脚印的谦卑，拉紧了纤绳，也塑造了心魂。

闽南真猛士，不与自然角力，只和自己较劲。

When all teams are congregated, people welcome King Renfu out of the temple with a palanquin. It is then that the lantern parade officially starts. The order of appearance of the lantern teams is determined by lots drawn at the temple by the heads of the lantern teams. The majestic palanquin of King Renfu staying in the middle and under the escort of the many lantern teams is carried by the team leaders. Taking the lead are four torches accompanied by gongs, pipes, swords and flags and bringing up the rear are umbrellas, fans and a band of woodwind and percussion instruments.

Arranged in good order and looking like a long snake, the lantern teams must first march three laps around the vast field in front of the temple, imitating the movement of a golden snake shedding its skin, signifying the beginning of the new year and the revival of everything.

After this grand ceremony, the lantern teams are allowed to march to the Hong family temple to pay their respect and parade around the temple. Then the lantern teams of each branch return to their own villages to welcome the parade around the whole town. Whenever the parade passes a house, the family will burn joss paper and set off firecrackers in front of their door to "welcome the lanterns". And the heads of the lantern teams enjoy the privilege of "keeping the lanterns", that is, they can have the palanquin of King Renfu stopped in front of their houses for a while when they burn joss sticks and make vows. The pronunciation of "lantern" is similar to that of "son", so welcoming the lanterns and keeping the lanterns signify an increase in family size.

After the tour around the whole town, only one lantern team is left to escort King Renfu back to the temple, where the head of the team burns incense and says the prayers and thus complete the mission of the year. Then, a respected elder tosses a pair of half-moon shaped bamboo plaques as a form of divination and decides the heads of next year's lantern teams. And this brings the annual Baba Deng Lantern Parade to a successful close.

The Baba Deng Lantern Parade of Yingdu Town reproduces the scene of old-time barge haulers towing boats along Yingxi Creek, offering a unique perspective on the prosperity of the inland river transport along the ancient Maritime Silk Road in Quanzhou. The power and strength it presents signify that the people here can bend to life but they will never bow to hardship. Step by step, they pull the ropes tight and grasp their fates in their own hands.

A true warrior in Southern Fujian does not wrestle with nature, but only with himself.

长长的灯龙。（视觉中国供图）

An endless stream of lanterns. (Courtesy of VCG.COM)

石狮端午闽台对渡习俗：蚶江鹿港对渡忙，海上泼水此日欢

“欢喜船入港，我君走船人，蚶江与鹿港，对渡来通航……欢喜船入港，两岸心相同，盼君早归航，泼水喜团圆。” 一首泉州民谣《欢喜船入港》，把盛大的闽台对渡和海上泼水情景描绘得有声有色。

若说十年修得同船渡，那么，这两岸声势浩大的对渡，又该修多少年？一方对渡碑为世人揭示了时间轴。原来蚶江海上泼水传统已存在五六百年之久，最早见于明，盛行于清。据《新建蚶江海防官署碑记》（载于对渡碑，系福建省省级文物保护单位）：“蚶江为泉州总口，与台湾鹿仔港对渡，大小商渔，往来利涉。其视鹿仔港直户庭耳。利之所在，群趋若鹜。”斯时蚶江作为大陆与台湾通商通航的中心码头，行郊百余家，对渡运输船只三百余艘，海上交通贸易繁荣兴盛。

岁月无情，乡情不变。即便到了今天，蚶江与台湾鹿港两地民众仍旧习惯在端午节身着节日盛装，于海面竞舟追逐泼水，人们视此水为“圣水情雨”，认为其可驱邪消灾，带来吉祥和海上安宁。欢乐的互动也使两地人民得以倾吐思念、交融情谊，从而使这血浓于水的两岸同乐泼水欢活动代代相传，绵延不断，成为全国乃至世界仅此一绝的民俗。

盛大的闽台对渡活动现场。（陈英杰 摄）
The grand scene of the Fujian-Taiwan Sea-Crossing activity. (Photo by Chen Yingjie)

Fujian-Taiwan Sea-Crossing Custom in Hanjiang, Shishi During the Dragon Boat Festival

"There is a direct shipping link between Hanjiang and Lukang and I am so happy to see the joy boat enters the harbor for my husband is a seafarer...Hurrah! The joy boat enters the harbor and I am so happy that the people on both sides of the Taiwan Strait are of the same mind. Hope my dearest can return early and join us in this Seawater-Splashing Festival and enjoy the happy reunion." Fujian-Taiwan Sea-Crossing Custom and Hanjiang Seawater-Splashing Festival are so movingly portrayed in a Quanzhou folk ballad, *Joy Boat Harbor*.

Starting in the Ming Dynasty and prevailing in the Qing Dynasty, Hanjiang Seawater-Splashing Festival has a history of about five or six hundred years. As is recorded in the inscription on the stone monument commonly known as Sea-Crossing Stele, a historical and cultural site protected at the provincial level, "Hanjiang is the main port for Quanzhou's trade with Taiwan. The direct shipping link between Hanjiang and Lukang greatly facilitates and promotes trade between the two sides and brings in huge profits." With over a hundred trade associations and three hundred cargo ships going back and forth, Hanjiang witnessed the great prosperity of maritime transportation and trade between Taiwan and the mainland at that time.

Despite the passage of time, the love for one's hometown remains steadfast. Even today, the people of Hanjiang in Shishi and Lukang in Taiwan are still used to wearing festive costumes, racing boats and splashing water over one another at sea during the Dragon Boat Festival. The water that is considered sacred is believed to be able to drive away evil spirits and bring good luck and peace on sea. The joyful interaction allows people of the two places to communicate their feelings and deepen their friendship, allowing the tradition of seawater-splashing to be passed down from generation to generation and become a unique folk custom in the country and even in the world.

蚶江位于石狮北部的泉州湾南岸，自有此活动以来，历代总是全情投入，《石狮市志》（二十五卷）载："农历五月初五为端午节……蚶江有海上泼水活动。是日，各乡各里的人涌向蚶江海滨，乘上小船，拿着戽斗、水桶盛水泼向对船上的人，互相嬉戏。"

除泼水外，两岸同胞还有一些共同的祭祀活动，如祭江、放水灯、祭五王爷等。王爷信仰是闽台两地特有的信俗，五月初五又是王爷生日，这一天，蚶江和台湾多个地方都要举行放王爷船仪式。

仁者乐山，智者乐水。逐水而居的闽南儿女深知水的蕴藉，水的丰盈。对渡泼水，泼向大地，泼向长空，泼向明天，泼向远方，这是乡愁的洗礼，更是圣洁的甘霖。

Hanjiang River lies in the north of Shishi on the south bank of Quanzhou Bay. Since the start of this activity, people have always been fully engaged in it. According to the *Local Gazetteer of Shishi* (Vol. 25), "The Dragon Boat Festival falls on the fifth day of the fifth lunar month, and there's the seawater-splashing activity in Hanjiang. On this day, people from various towns and villages flock to the seashore of Hanjiang River, get on small boats and use washbasins and buckets to throw water at people on other boats to offer blessings for safe sea voyages and enjoy the festivities with one another."

In addition to throwing water, compatriots on both sides of the Taiwan Strait also share some rituals such as offering sacrifices to the river, launching of water lanterns and worshiping Ong Yah, the guardian deity believed to stop diseases from spreading and bestow good fortune. The belief in Ong Yah is a custom unique to both Fujian and Taiwan, and on the fifth day of the fifth lunar month, which is also the birthday of Ong Yah, the Ong Yah Boat Launching Ceremony takes place in various locations across Hanjiang and Taiwan.

As the Chinese saying goes, a benevolent man enjoys the mountains and a wise man enjoys the water. Living by the water, the people of Southern Fujian are well aware of the richness and abundance of water. The Dragon Boat Festival is also the Seawater-Splashing Festival for them. And the water they throw at each others' boats, the earth and the sky is the attachment to their hometown as well as their blessings for safe voyages and peaceful life.

对渡泼水欢。（陈小阳 摄）

People from both sides of the Taiwan Strait are enjoying the sea-crossing and water-splashing activity. (Photo by Chen Xiaoyang)

安海嗦啰嗹习俗：
端午奇俗嗦啰嗹，龙王采莲采四方

“江南可采莲，莲叶何田田。”朱自清先生的现代美文《荷塘月色》，遥遥地呼应着《汉乐府》里描述的千年传统。莲的物语，就是中国人的心事。由此，才生发出如此的礼俗与赞颂。

其实，每个人心中，都有个荷塘梦。关于这个梦，却是泉州人最浪漫。若非如此，当地人便不会把采莲活动吟成了曲。那歌谣中，还有一种谜一般的吉祥语，叫作“嗦啰嗹”。一般人以为它是民间俚语，事实上，它来自佛教梵语，代表吉祥如意。

采莲这一习俗源自汉代，而那清新自然的《采莲曲》，则是泉州晋江安海嗦啰嗹最原始的母版。唐末五代时期，闽王王审知悉心维系中原民俗，每年五月莲花盛开时节，都携带宫眷泛舟赏莲，并命宫廷乐师吹奏《采莲曲》。此风后来渐渐传入民间，流传于泉州一带，成为一种百姓娱乐活动。

有意思的是，最初泉州的采莲活动是在农历五月初一进行，至清朝中晚期，演变为与纪念爱国诗人屈原的端午节活动（农历五月初五）合并举行。同时，五月初五这天也与泉州民间所谓的龙王诞辰有关，于是又加入了龙王崇拜的内容，衍生出一种涵盖采莲祈福、纪念屈原、拜龙赐福等内容的盛大活动。

安海嗦啰嗹习俗表演。（陈起拓 摄）
A performance of Anhai Suo Luo Lian. (Photo by Chen Qituo)

Anhai Suo Luo Lian (the Lotus-Picking Ritual)

Rising from the mud and blooming in exquisite beauty, the lotus flower, in traditional Chinese culture, symbolizes not only the holy seat of Buddha but also purity of the mind and spirit, as well as personal growth and enlightenment. That's why the lotus has always been an important theme in Chinese literature, be it ancient poems or modern prose.

The Chinese express their love for the lotus flower in various ways, the most romantic of which must be the Lotus-Picking Ritual in Quanzhou featuring singing and dancing. In singing, the performers keep chanting an enigmatic auspicious phrase "Suo Luo Lian", which is thought to be a folk slang but in fact it originates from Buddhist Sanskrit and stands for good fortune.

The custom of lotus-picking traces its history to the Han Dynasty, and the fresh and natural *Lotus-Picking Song* is the most original version of the "Suo Luo Lian" chant of Anhai Town in Jinjiang, the satellite city of Quanzhou. During the late Tang and Five Dynasties period, Wang Shenzhi, the vassal king of the Min Kingdom (now Southern Fujian) made it a point to maintain the folk customs of the Central Plains, and every year in lunar May, when lotus flowers were in full bloom, he would take his queen and concubines out on a boat to enjoy the flowers and order the court musicians to play the *Lotus-Picking Song*. This practice gradually spread among the common people and became a popular pastime for the people around Quanzhou.

Interestingly, the activity of Lotus-Picking in Quanzhou was originally held on the first day of the fifth lunar month. And in the middle of the late Qing Dynasty, it was combined with the Dragon Boat Festival which commemorates the patriotic poet Qu Yuan, who threw himself into the river on the fifth day of the same month. Besides, as that very day is also the birthday of the Dragon King in Quanzhou culture, the worship of the Dragon King was incorporated into the festival so that it became a grand event which includes Lotus-Picking to pray for blessings, commemoration of Qu Yuan and the worship of Dragon King.

若到晋江安海看热闹，五月初五这天，你必须起个大早，方能一饱眼福：这是一行经过装扮的队伍，整个队伍以头戴清兵笠、手撑长杆艾旗的醉步汉子为前导，敲锣鼓、奏管弦的队伍两旁是肩挑生猪脚、草鞋和尿壶酒，手打破锣的铺兵及头包乌布、身着红衣红裤、手提鲜花篮、脚穿绣花鞋的男扮花婆。龙王头则由四个壮汉抬行，装束威严，角缠红布，两眼圆睁，海口张裂，龙须长伸，震慑四方。每到一家，旗手如醉似癫地冲入厅堂，挥动艾旗在梁间拂扫，高诵“龙神采莲来，兴旺大发财”等祝祷辞。男扮花婆走科步，与旗手对舞一番后，向户主馈送鲜花，表示龙王神留下福禄吉祥，户主接过鲜花即回赠红包答谢，并在门口放鞭炮叩送龙王神，整个场面喜庆且热闹。

习俗是另一种天性，总有一种久违的亲切和温暖。莲的物语，诗的雅致，龙的祝福，在这里“一举三得”。倘若你来，它们会毫不犹豫地敞开心扉，在五月，邀你以一夏的盛情。

行进中的采莲队。（陈起拓 摄）
A team of lotus pickers on the move. (Photo by Chen Qituo)

To experience the festival in Anhai Town for yourself, you must get up early on the fifth day of the fifth lunar month. It involves a lively procession with people dressed in costume. Led by a staggering fake drunkard wearing a bamboo hat of the style of the Qing Dynasty soldiers and holding a tall flag, the procession is made up of a band of gongs, drums and orchestras in the middle and patrolmen and women clowns played by men on either side. The patrolmen carrying raw pig's feet, straw shoes and large pottery jugs of wine on their shoulders are striking broken gongs at the same time, while the men acting as women clowns wrap their heads with black cloth, wear red blouses, red pants and embroidered shoes, and carry baskets of flowers with them. Carried by four strong men is the head of the awe-inspiring Dragon King adorned in a majestic outfit. With red cloth around his horns, his eyes and mouth are wide open and his beard stretches out. At each house, the flag bearers rush into the hall feverishly, waving the flags, sweeping between beams and chanting prayers of good luck and prosperity. The men who act as clown women dance with the flag bearers for a while and then present flowers to the householder as a sign of good fortune and prosperity left by the Dragon King. After receiving the flowers, the householder gives a red envelop in return and send the Dragon King off by setting off firecrackers, making the whole scene festive and lively.

Custom is second nature, the thought of which always warms the hearts. Picking lotus, commemorating the patriotic poet Qu Yuan and worshiping the Dragon King, the festival offers a three in one feast. Visitors are welcomed to experience the warm hospitality of the festival in the beautiful month of lunar May.

惠安女服饰：
封建头，民主肚；节约衫，浪费裤

潮水不舍昼夜，抚拍着这片大地，卷起千堆雪。海的女儿，一肩挑起顽石，一肩挑起岁月。夕阳剪剪风，斗笠下的眼睛，远眺着天际，良人的孤帆远影，拖长无尽的相思。那一袭特殊的装束，兀自站立成海边的风景。她们是惠安女，辨识度超高的一个女性群体。“封建头，民主肚；节约衫，浪费裤”，这独一份的古早时尚，让她们从头美到脚。

惠安女服饰是流传于泉州惠安一带独特的妇女服饰，可分为崇武、山霞和小岞、净峰两个类型。上衣有大裾衫、接袖衫，后逐渐演变为缀做衫、节约衫。裤子有大折裤、黑丝绸裤、黑布裤、蓝布裤等。饰物则包括百褶边裙、贴背和褡裢、腰中、袖套、银腰链及小竹篾篮等。发型有未婚和已婚之严格区别，婚后又有盛装发型和便装发型之分。头饰和首饰有黄斗笠、花头巾、银手镯、金戒指等。鞋则有凤冠鞋、踩跷鞋及拖鞋。

惠安女是大海的女儿。（陈英杰 摄）
Hui'an women, daughters of the sea. (Photo by Chen Yingjie)

Costumes of Hui'an Women

A visit to the seaside villages of Hui'an, one can never miss the sight of women with bamboo hats doing manual labor. They are Hui'an women, a highly recognizable group of women, whose unique costumes are exceptionally beautiful and jokingly described as "a feudal head, a democratic belly, saving the jacket and wasting the pants." The "feudal head" refers to the headwear of Hui'an females—namely the colorful kerchief and yellow bamboo hat. Since females have to cover their faces with the kerchief and wear a round bamboo hat on the head, they leave only half of the face visible. "Saving the jacket" means that the upper outer of Hui'an Women's Costumes is rather short (just above their waists) and the cuff is contracted up to the middle forearm, which doesn't cost much fabric. The "democratic belly" means that the tight and short upper outer of females would not conceal the navels of them at labor, which reflects the democratic principle of the society. "Wasting the pants" means the loose and large bottom, however, costs more.

Unique to Hui'an County of Quanzhou, Hui'an Women's Costumes, geographically speaking, can be divided into two types, those from Chongwu Town and Shanxia Town and those from Xiaozuo Town and Jingfeng Town. The length of the tops of the costumes has varied over time, from kneel-length, to waist-length and then crop-top, while the wide-legged pants vary from black silk ones or black or blue cloth ones. Accessories include plaited sashes for ceremonious occasions, waistcoats for keeping warm in autumn and winter, embroidered pouches, aprons for housework or farmwork, oversleeves, silver belts for married women, and small bamboo baskets. Married and unmarried women have distinct hairstyles. For married women, there's also the difference between the formal hairstyle and the casual one. Other accessories include headwear and jewellery such as yellow bamboo hats, flowered headscarves, silver bracelets and gold rings. Shoes include red woolen embroidered wedding shoes, red satin embroidered shoes for ceremonious occasions and slippers for daily work.

在惠安女的美丽面前，任何一种试图用现代服饰理念诠释它全部内涵的冲动，或许都是徒劳。有人类学者、民俗专家言之凿凿，这是已经消失的古代百越族群所遗存下的古老美学记忆，同时又集海洋文化、中原文化等装束哲学之大成，绸缪碰撞，多元交融，淬成独特的“惠安风”。

细看其服装纹样，包含篮纹、绳纹、斜线纹、云雷纹和附加堆纹，竟与考古学家从崇武大岞山新石器时代文化遗址地表采集到的陶片上的纹饰有着天然的吻合。更有考古学家发现，惠安女服饰色彩框架的形成源自原始的族徽和图腾崇拜。历史上，惠东人群是来自古百越民族的一个支流，民间传其为闽南十八峒之蝴蝶峒的后裔，蝴蝶是其原始的族徽和崇拜对象，惠安女服饰因此在服饰色彩上追求蝴蝶的艳丽华贵，也喜用蝴蝶图案的种种纹样，如头饰中的蝴蝶造型等。

探究惠安女服饰文化，更不能忽略其海洋生活元素，半岛、海岬的自然环境具象化地融合在其视觉效果上，强烈的美学主体意识保证其不受社会主流服饰和其他民族服饰的冲击而世代传承。但美学系统本身也会随着主体意识的迭代而发生丰富的变化。随着物质生活的富足，新时代的惠安女更愿意在服饰花样上精雕细琢，有时个人饰品的数量也由十几件达到上百件之多。她们像童话里归来的海的女儿，和大海一起延伸着浪花呢喃的诗意，美得不可方物，美得落落大方。

身着传统服饰的小小惠安女。（陈英杰 摄）
Little Hui'an girls in their traditional costumes. (Photo by Chen Yingjie)

In the face of the beautiful Costumes of Hui'an Women, any attempts to interpret them with modern ideas of clothes will probably be futile. Anthropologists and experts in folklore, however, are convinced that the costumes originated from the long vanished Minyue tribes in ancient times and evolved with influences from Central Plains culture and local sea culture before the unique Hui'an style was eventually formed.

A closer look at the decorative designs, including basket-weave patterns, rope patterns, diagonal lines, cloud & thunder patterns and overlapped patterns, one can easily find that they are entirely consistent with the patterns on pottery collected by archaeologists from the Neolithic Cultural Site of Dazuo Mountain in Chongwu Town. Some archaeologists have even found that the color schemes of Hui'an women's clothing originate from the primitive clan crest and totem worship. Historically, the people of Huidong (Eastern Hui'an) were from a tribe of the ancient Baiyue nationality and were said to be descendants of the Butterfly Cave, one of the eighteen settlements of the ethnic minorities in Southern Fujian whose clan emblem and totem worship was the butterfly. As a result, the color of Hui'an women's clothing is as bright and rich as that of the butterfly and for decorative patterns, they have a special preference for various patterns of the butterfly, such as their butterfly-shaped headwears.

To explore Hui'an women's costume culture, one cannot ignore elements of marine life. The natural environment of the peninsula and the cape is figuratively integrated in its visual effect, and the strong aesthetic consciousness ensures that it will be passed down from generation to generation despite the impact of mainstream social costumes and other national costumes. However, the aesthetic system is subject to rich changes as time changes. With an increasing abundance of the material life, Hui'an women are more willing to elaborate on the patterns of their clothing, and the number of their personal accessories reaches from a dozen to hundreds. One-of-a-kind in the whole country, the Costumes of Hui'an Women make these daughters of the sea stunningly beautiful and graceful.

蟳埔女习俗：
阿母头髻顶，素馨花开了八百年

“十里不同风，百里不同俗”，告别惠安女，驱车沿泉州沿海大通道往南数十里，便可邂逅蟳埔女。

她们盘起一头乌黑的秀发，用一只坚实的骨笄横穿固定。她们头戴簪花围，让姹紫嫣红的鲜花团簇着开满高昂的头颅。

盛装之下，怒放的生命，夺人眼球。任谁初次得见，都会感觉有一股异域文化气息扑面而来，而这却是泉州蟳埔一带最寻常见到的女子装扮。海风、闽南风、生活风，每一阵风都跨越这身装束翩跹而至，让人不免追寻其脚步，去探究这番风情背后的传奇。

传统的蟳埔人基本生活在蚵壳厝里，这是最具特色的闽南民居。据考证，蟳埔蚵壳厝的大蚵壳并非泉州原产，而是由宋元时期古刺桐港的远洋商船空舱返航时为压舱而运抵。由此，世人总是戏称，蟳埔女是把海洋文化戴在了头上，把自己又住进了海洋里。

风情万种的蟳蜅女发式。（王福平 摄）
The fascinating and charming hairdo of Xunpu women. (Photo by Wang Fuping)

Custom of Xunpu Women

Customs of different areas can vary greatly even though they are not really far apart. Bidding farewell to Hui'an women and driving some 5 kilometers south along the coastal road of Quanzhou, you'll surely be attracted by the hairdo of Xunpu women.

They wear their hair in a bun, hold their hairstyle in place with a bone hairpin, and then put garlands of flowers around the bun.

The garlands of blooming flowers are very beautiful and eye-catching. Whoever sees this for the first time will be impressed by the exoticism, but, as a matter of fact, it is the most common way of dressing for a woman in the neighborhood of Xunpu Village in Quanzhou. The unique hairdo combines elements of sea culture, Southern Fujian culture and traditional folk custom of garments, creating a fascinating cultural phenomenon.

Traditionally, villagers in Xunpu live in oyster shell houses, which is one of the most distinctive folk houses in Southern Fujian. Research has shown that the large oyster shells used for these houses are not native to Quanzhou, but were brought in as ballast with the return of the empty ocean-going merchant ships to the ancient port of Zayton during the Song and Yuan dynasties. As a result, people often humorously comment that the women of Xunpu are wearing the sea culture on their heads and taking up residence in the sea.

承载岁月的蟳埔村蚵壳厝。（成冬冬 摄）
An age-old oyster shell house in Xunpu. (Photo by Cheng Dongdong)

细看下，蟳埔女的装束之独特，主要体现在头饰风情、服饰风韵和不事雕饰的粗脚头等元素上，尽显渔女原生态。“尘世难逢开口笑，菊花须插满头归”，但蟳埔女所戴的鲜花比菊花罕见得多，它们多来自附近的云麓村，许多人甚至闻所未闻，即素馨花（泉州话称“素娘花”）、含笑花、粗糠花。据考证，南宋时，该村原是泉州市舶司提举阿拉伯人蒲寿庚的私家别墅——云麓花园，而园中的茉莉花、素馨花等正是从波斯湾引进的特殊品种，属于地地道道的舶来花品。而蟳埔女发式里的骨笄则保留了古代“骨针安发”的本意，系全国独有的头饰活化石。

孤阴不生，独阳不长，蟳埔文化的风头，不能全被女人们抢走。试看蟳埔男性的装束，也是尽显个性。首先是蟳埔男性上衣的直裾，正如《师古注》所言：“裾亦傲也。”直裾的意义，即当地男子性格磊落耿直，不屈不挠。作为呼应，当地女子的衣襟则为弯裾。这一美的对称，巧妙地展示出蟳埔人男刚女柔、刚柔相济的性格特点。

与装束相映成趣的礼俗则更令人耳目一新。至今蟳埔仍保留着许许多多的传统习俗，诸如别具一格的半夜出嫁婚俗、完整浩大的妈祖巡香民俗。后者通常在农历正月廿九举行，对于全村来说，这是一年中最热闹的节日之一。见识过那场面的人，才能理解何谓“信仰在于斯，虔诚在于斯”。

衣冠南渡的中原先贤砥砺八闽大地，随着时间的推移，又在海丝之路上迎接各种文化的交流融合。穿在身上的礼俗，便是文明行走在大地时最美的移动符号。

华夏之韵，文化悠长；服饰之好，丝路回响。

妈祖巡香民俗活动现场，万千人中的回眸一笑。（陈英杰 摄）
A woman, amid the thousands of devotees in the grand sacrificial ceremony for the sea Goddess, Mazu, looked back and smiled at the camera. (Photo by Chen Yingjie)

The uniqueness of Xunpu women's costumes lies in the headwear, the hairdo and the clothing style which are typical of the fisherwomen. Flowers usually worn by women of Xunpu are frangipani, michelia and groundsel, which are not commonly seen and the names of which are something unheard of by most people. They are mostly from a nearby village, Yunlu Village, which is believed to be the private villa of Pu Shougeng, a super rich Arabian sea merchant who served as the superintendent of Shi Bo Si (Maritime Trade Office) during the Southern Song Dynasty. Such flowers as jasmine and frangipani found in his garden are special varieties imported from the Persian Gulf. Even the hairpins used by Xunpu women are of historical meaning. In ancient China, hairpins used to be favorites of men when they presented gifts to their lovers and women often took them as tokens of love. Xunpu women preserve the custom of using a bone hairpin to fix the hair, thus making it a living fossil of headdress unique in China.

It takes both men and women to make the world complete. The culture of Xunpu can't do without men. Men express their individuality through their clothing as well. First of all, the front of Xunpu men's clothing is straight, symbolizing that local men are straightforward and unyielding in character. As an echo, the front of local women's clothing is curving. This beautiful symmetry subtly demonstrates the perfect complement of masculinity and femininity of Xunpu men and women.

The rituals that go hand in hand with the costumes are even more refreshing, as there kept in Xunpu are many traditional customs, such as the unique midnight wedding ceremony and the grand sacrificial ceremony for the sea Goddess, Mazu. It falls on the 29th day of the first lunar month and is one of the liveliest festivals of the year for the whole village. Only those who have seen it with their own eyes understand how sincere and devoted one can be to his belief.

Going through great hardships and overcoming various difficulties, the noble classes from the Central Plains moved southward to Fujian Province during the Jin and Tang dynasties. After that they were confronted with the exchange and integration of various cultures brought with the trade on the Maritime Silk Road. Costumes for different occasions are beautiful moving symbols of civilization.

Clothing has always been an indispensable part in the long history of Chinese culture, and the traditional costumes of Xunpu women undoubtedly make a distinctively beautiful scene of Quanzhou, the starting point of the Maritime Silk Road.

清水祖师信俗：
庇护垂爱九百年，神缘缔结东南亚

他的全球信众逾亿。每年春风吹拂的日子，便是他下山绕境、庇护四方的时候。九百多年来，人们始终相信，只要他的神迹一到，就会风调雨顺、国泰民安。

清水祖师，一位因善成佛、对老百姓“营以种种方便”的民间神祇，在闽粤浙台等地及东南亚各国华人社区有着极其深广的信仰影响力。在世界闽南文化圈，因着对清水祖师的同一信仰，纵使隔着千山万水，人们也每每相邀成群，共赴信俗发源地——泉州安溪清水岩，虔诚叩首，祈愿求福。

始建于北宋元丰六年（1083）的清水岩坐落在安溪城郊西北 16 千米处的蓬莱山。说来神奇，那里长年云雾缥缈，仿若人间仙境，故享有“蓬莱仙境”之美誉。更绝之处在于，构建于宋代的建筑清水殿是中国唯一的“帝”字形寺庙，让每一个朝圣者都油然心生敬意。别样造化别样景，清水岩的人文景观与自然景观独具一格，有学者统计，岩上现有宋代文物胜迹 29 处，元代 1 处，明代 8 处，清代 5 处，近代拓展、恢复 23 处。其中，南宋遗物岩图碑正是南宋初期为兴修清水岩而打下的“石头图纸”，可谓举世无双。

清水殿“帝”字形建筑群。（陈起拓 摄）
The Qingshui Temple complex built in the shape of the Chinese character “帝”. (Photo by Chen Qituo)

Belief in Master Qingshui, the Buddhist Monk

He has more than 100 million devotees worldwide. Every year when spring arrives, it is his time to come down the mountain for a patrol and bring blessings to people. For more than 900 years, people have always believed that with the mighty acts of his, there will be good weather and peace for people.

Master Qingshui, a folk deity who attained Buddhahood by virtue of his kindness of providing common people with all kinds of convenience, has a very deep and wide religious influence in the Chinese communities of regions like Fujian, Guangdong, Zhejiang, Taiwan and some Southeast Asian countries. Every year, many devotees of Southern Fujian origin all over the world, however far apart they are, will go on a pilgrimage to Qingshuiyan Temple in Anxi County in Quanzhou, the birthplace of their shared faith.

First built in 1083 during the Northern Song Dynasty, Qingshuiyan scenic area is located in Penglai Mountain, a suburb district 16 kilometers northwest of Anxi County. It is a magical place where clouds and mists drift in and out all year round, as if it were heaven on earth, and therefore enjoys the reputation of "Wonderland Penglai". What is even more amazing and awe-inspiring is that the age-old temple complex, Qingshui Temple, is the only temple in China built in the shape of the Chinese character "帝" (emperor). The cultural and natural landscapes of Qingshuiyan are unique in their own way. According to the statistics of scholars, among the cultural relics and historic sites in the scenic spot, 29 are from the Song Dynasty, 1 is from the Yuan Dynasty, 8 are from the Ming Dynasty, 5 are from the Qing Dynasty and 23 are from the recent expansion and restoration. The most precious and unique one, however, is the Stone Map Tablet from the early years of the Southern Song Dynasty which was carved for the construction of Qingshuiyan.

自宋朝以来，清水祖师信俗已经跨越了多个朝代，流传至今，仍香火鼎盛。人们更津津乐道的是他那动人的传奇故事。清水祖师原名陈应（又作陈昭应），于宋仁宗景祐四年（1037）农历正月初六诞生于永春小姑乡，自幼落发为僧，法号普足，又称麻章上人，为大宋名僧。宋神宗元丰六年（1083），清溪（即安溪）、永春一带大旱，乡人请他祈雨，立刻甘霖普降，因此得尊称“清水祖师”。宋徽宗政和三年（1113）陈浩然撰《清水祖师本传》，称其广造桥亭、多植竹木、祷佛弭灾，足迹远及汀、漳，声名广披闽南。

正因“祖师生前，德高道深，多行善事”，其逝后，“百姓感恩，崇奉为佛，香火旺盛”。每逢病疫或亢旱，乡人必恭抬其像，祈求襄助。百姓赋予清水祖师神奇甚至神秘的色彩，宋廷则顺应民意，敕赐其“昭应广惠慈济善利大师”徽号，八字纶音，享誉至极。

泉流法雨，情超物外。经数百年演变，清水祖师信俗内容日益丰富，成为影响广泛的闽南信俗文化遗产，总体可分为祭祀、卜签两大类，而祭祀活动亦具有鲜明的民俗性。值得一提的是，其药签文化中，还蕴藏着中国不可多得的中医药宝贵遗产，于世罕见。

何必沧海，此山即是蓬莱；千峰化境，此泉可润禅心。在至真至善面前，普罗大众选择用头点赞，用信念加持。

台北市三峡祖师庙主祀清水祖师。（中新图片 供图）
Sanxia Ancestral Temple in Taipei worships Master Qingshui. (Courtesy of CNSphoto.com)

The Belief in Master Qingshui has spanned many dynasties since the Song Dynasty and remains popular to this day. Legends of him never fail to fascinate people. His secular name being Chen Ying (also Chen Zhaoying), and his Buddhist name being Puzu (also Mazhang), Master Qingshui was an eminent monk of the Song Dynasty. Born in Yongchun County on the sixth day of the first lunar month in 1037, he became a monk at an early age. In 1083, when there was a severe drought in the area of Qingxi (now Anxi) and Yongchun, the villagers entreated him to pray for rain and immediately the rain fell, so he was respectfully called Master Qingshui (clear water). In 1113, Chen Haoran wrote *A Biography of Master Qingshui*, saying that with footprints covering as far as Changting and Zhangzhou, he built many bridges and pavilions, planted many bamboos and trees, prayed to Buddha to relieve disasters and gained a wide reputation in Southern Fujian.

It is because of "the great virtue and good deeds of Master Qingshui during his lifetime" that after his death, "People were still grateful and worshiped him as a Buddha who later attracted more and more followers." Whenever there's an epidemic or a drought, villagers would carry his statue from the temple and paraded around the whole village, hoping that he would dispel the evil. The people regarded Master Qingshui as imbued with divine and mystical power so in response to public opinion, the Song Dynasty emperor bestowed upon him an eight-character title of great honor, Master Zhaoying Guanghui Ciji Shanli (a very effective, generous, kind and compassionate master named Zhaoying).

Throughout the centuries, the content and customs of the Belief in Master Qingshui have been constantly enriched so that it has become a widely influential cultural heritage of Southern Fujian. It can be divided into two main categories: rituals and divination, the former of which are mostly folk customs with distinctive features. What is worth mentioning is that its medical prescription oracle, which is rare in the world, is of great value in the heritage of Chinese medicine.

The essence of religious belief is the pursuit of the highest truth and the highest good. And this is why Master Qingshui, from a mortal being to a deity, has inspired countless people and attracted more and more followers over the years.

送王船：
攘灾保境漂彩船，填平疫海不扬波

它绝非普罗米修斯盗取的文明天火，亦非奥林匹斯山点燃的运动圣火，更非费翔扭动身体嘶吼的“冬天里的一把火”。

但这把火，却火遍闽南几百年。

它送瘟神，消灾厄，因而火得有道理，火得得人心。

它就是闽南献祭王爷的重要民俗活动——送王船，也称为送“瘟船”“彩船”。

任何一种地方民俗的形成，无不与其生存环境之复杂密切相关。泉州属亚热带季风气候区，潮湿闷热，历史上自然灾害频繁，其中尤以瘟疫为害最甚。为保境安民，信众依托王爷神力，以送王船的形式祈求驱除瘟疫、消解厄运，借此增强人们抗御自然灾害的精神力量。都说“人世维艰，求之于天”，这可以看作一种天人合一的生存智慧。

送王船活动颇有历史渊源。据清乾隆《泉州府志·卷二十·风俗》记载：“端阳……五月，是月无定日，里社攘灾，先日延道设醮，至期以纸为大舟，送五方瘟神，凡百器用皆备，陈鼓乐、仪仗、百戏，送水次焚之。近竟有以木舟具真器，用以浮于海者。”

泉州石狮蚶江“金再兴”号王爷船巡海仪式。（视觉中国 供图）
The boat "Jin Zai Xing" set afloat during the Ong Chun launching ceremony held in Hanjiang Town of Shishi, Quanzhou. (Courtesy of VCG.COM)

The Ong Chun/ Wangchuan/ Wangkang Ceremony

It is by no means the fire of civilization Prometheus stole for men, nor is it the sacred fire of sport lit on Mount Olympus, nor is it the fire sung in the popular song *Fire in Winter* by Fei Xiang, a Chinese pop singer.

This particular form of fire, however, has been popular in Southern Fujian for centuries.

It is intended for sending plagues away and eliminating disasters, and is therefore well-justified and popular.

The Ong Chun/ Wangchuan/ Wangkang Ceremony is an important folk custom of worshiping Ong Yah, a deity believed to protect people and their lands from disasters in Southern Fujian.

The formation of any folk custom is closely related to the complexity of its environment. Quanzhou is located in a subtropical monsoon climate zone, which is humid and sultry, and has historically been prone to natural disasters, especially plagues. Followers of Ong Yah believed that they could rely on the divine power of him to expel the plague and dispel bad luck by building, launching and burning Ong Yah's barge (a wooden or paper-made model) symbolizing the evil. As the saying goes, "If life in the world is hard, one should seek help from gods." In the old days, it was in this way that people's spiritual strength in resisting natural disasters was enhanced. And to pray for the harmony between man and nature was probably a survival wisdom.

The Ong Chun Ceremony has a long history. According to *Local Chronicles of Quanzhou Prefecture, Vol. 20, Customs* compiled between 1736 and 1796, "Around the Dragon Boat Festival in the fifth lunar month, the Ong Chun Ceremony was under preparation. Villagers would invite the Taoist monks to perform a ritual several days before the paper boat symbolizing the plague and bad luck was made. When the day came, with the accompaniment of drums, bands and various folk performances, the boat would be launched and burned. And sometimes wooden models were used."

泉郡富美宫是全世界送王船文化的发祥地，也是最具盛名的送王船仪式所在地。它始建于明正德年间，主祀萧太傅萧王爷，配祀廿四司、文武尊王等。富美宫所造的王船因体形大，可漂至台湾，甚至东南亚地区，所以声名远扬。据相关记载，自清代以来，迎富美宫送出的王船的，就有台湾新竹富美宫，台湾苗栗外埔合兴宫，台湾台中罗施港（现名大安港）和安宫，台湾嘉义东石港先天宫、外伞顶洲等。

明清以来，由于王爷崇拜在泉州府所辖地区特别盛行，随着泉州移民的足迹，也在海内外得到广泛传播，其分灵遍布闽南、台湾地区以及马来西亚、新加坡等国家。

送王船文化发祥地——泉州富美宫。（许兆恺 摄）
Fumei Temple in Quanzhou, the birthplace of the world's Ong Chun culture. (Photo by Xu Zhaokai)

First built between 1506 and 1521 during the Ming Dynasty, Fumei Temple in Quanzhou is the birthplace of the world's Ong Chun culture as well as the most famous site of the Ong Chun Ceremony. Among the 27 Ong Yah (deities who were originally mortal beings) worshiped in the palace, the principal god is Xiao Wangzhi, a famous official of the Western Han Dynasty (220 B.C.—8 A.D.), and the rest are also highly respected figures who have made great contributions to the people and nation, including officials, officers and even doctors. The Ong Yah's barge made by Fumei Temple is famous for its large size and the ability to sail to Taiwan Province and even some Southeast Asian countries. Historical records indicate that during the Qing Dynasty, the worship of Ong Yah and Ong Chun Ceremony were introduced to Taiwan Province. Ever since then, many temples have been built to worship Ong Yah when people there found the Ong Yah's barges sent from Fumei Temple in Quanzhou. Among the list are Fumei Temple in Hsinchu, He-Sing Temple in Waipu, Miaoli, He'an Temple in Luoshi Port (now Da'an Port), Taichung, Xiantian Temple and Waisanding Sandbar in Dongshi, Chiayi.

Since the Ming and Qing dynasties, the worship of Ong Yah has been particularly popular in the areas under the jurisdiction of Quanzhou Prefecture, and it has also been introduced by migrants of Quanzhou to other regions such as Zhangzhou, Xiamen and Taiwan as well as some Southeast Asian countries including Malaysia and Singapore.

马来西亚送王船博物馆存有世界上最古老的送王船照片。（中新图片 供图）
Melaka Wangkang Museum houses the oldest photo of the Ong Chun Ceremony. (Courtesy of CNSphoto.com)

富美宫送王船的程序十分讲究。首先，须得卜筊、择吉请道士做醮之后，才能着手造王船。造毕，开始安置龙骨，举行祭礼、开斧。其后，便是迎王船、建醮环节，此时须进行醮会活动，祈求风调雨顺、国泰民安。前头工作都顺利进行完，才开始安放王船。安放过程中，要配备仪仗（大牌、凉伞、旌旗等），乐队（锣、鼓、弦管等），武器（刀、剑等），出海神像，供品及各种生活用品，还要做水醮祭海。礼毕，王船在富美渡头下水，由事先挑选好的几名水手身背王爷符箓，按王爷指定的时间起锚，从江下游驶出泉州湾后，停泊于祥芝海上，举行人神交接仪式，而后献祭，由水手按预定方向张帆起锚，然后焚化所背的符箓。最后这一把火点燃，整个仪式才算结束，人员离船上岸，王船随风逐浪漂向远方。

2020 年 12 月 17 日，联合国教科文组织将中国与马来西亚联合申报的“送王船——有关人与海洋可持续联系的仪式及相关实践”项目列入联合国教科文组织《人类非物质文化遗产代表作名录》。送王船传递着人们对先辈走向海洋的历史记忆，休现了人与自然和谐相处、尊重生命的理念，为推动包容性社会发展提供了丰富的文化对话资源；其承载的观察气象、潮汐、洋流等海洋知识和航海技术，是人们长期海上生产生活智慧的结晶；送王船被相关国家的社区视为共同遗产，是中华文化在海上丝绸之路沿线国家传播与融合的生动例证。

“坐地日行八万里，巡天遥看一千河。”王船悠悠，代天巡狩；里社靖安，旌旗高扬。古礼中承载的最重要的集体海洋记忆，比远方更远。

台湾省屏东县东港镇东隆宫“王船祭”活动烧王船。（中新图片 供图）
The boat burning scene of Ong Chun Ceremony held by Donglong Palace in Donggang Township, Pingtung County, Taiwan Province. (Courtesy of CNSphoto.com)

The process of the Ong Chun Ceremony is very elaborate. First, after the divination, an auspicious time must be selected to invite the Taoist monks to perform a rite of cosmic renewal before the making of a Ong Yah barge. The keel is placed upon the completion of the barge and a sacrificial rite and prayer ceremony is held. Afterwards, the barge is welcomed and another rite is held to pray for good weather for the crops and peace and prosperity for people. After the completion of all the previous work, there comes the launching of the Ong Yah barge, which requires an honor guard of large plaques, umbrellas and flags, a band of gongs, drums, strings and pipes, weapons such as knives and swords, statues of gods, offerings and various daily necessities, as well as a sacrificial rite to the sea. After the rituals, the Ong Yah barge is launched in Fumei Ferry. Several sailors selected in advance set off at the time specified in the divination, carrying the Ong Yah talismans on their backs. They sail out of Quanzhou Bay from the lower reaches of the river, stop over at the sea of Xiangzhi near Shishi, a satellite city of Quanzhou, hold a ceremony for the handover between man and God followed by the offering of sacrifices, after which they sail in the intended direction and then incinerate the talismans they carry. The burning brings the whole ceremony to a close and sailors leave the barge and go ashore while the barge drifting away with the wind and waves.

On December 17, 2020, the program "Ong Chun/ Wangchuan/ Wangkang Ceremony, rituals and related practices for maintaining the sustainable connection between man and the ocean", jointly nominated by China and Malaysia , was inscribed on the *Representative List of the Intangible Cultural Heritage of Humanity* by UNESCO. The ceremony, rituals and related practices evoke the historical memory of ancestors' ocean-going; honour the harmony between man and the ocean and respect for life; provide rich cultural dialogue resources for promoting the development of an inclusive society; its marine knowledge and navigation technology, such as observing meteorology, tides and ocean currents, are the crystallization of people's long-term wisdom in marine production and life; and that the ceremony's being regarded as a common heritage by the communities of the countries concerned is a vivid example of the spread and integration of Chinese culture in the countries along the Maritime Silk Road.

All sorrows and joys will become a thing of the past with the passage of time. The making, launching and burning of Ong Yah barges to get rid of plagues and bad luck is not only the most important collective memory of the sea but also the eternal hope of people for a peaceful and prosperous life.

通远王信俗：
第一海神佑天下，每岁舶司两祈风

沧海一声笑，滔滔两岸潮，这是真正的男神，唐宋以来中国第一代海神——通远王。

通远王俗名李元溥，四川人，唐玄宗天宝年间进士，著有《灵响》一书，官拜云南团练副使。后为逃避战乱弃官隐居，云游到南安、永春交界处的乐山，便结庐于此，修行二十余载羽化而去，乡人称其为“乐山王”。

升仙之后，“乐山老人”不甘寂寞，便开始大显神通，为当地人民做了许许多多的好事，属于唐宋版“感动中国”头条人物。据《南安县志·卷二·舆地志》记载：“唐咸通中，僧初建殿，取材于永春之乐山，遇一叟为之导……盖乐山之神焉，祠以祀之。水旱疫疠，海舶祈风，辄见应……”因屡显灵异，民间尊其为“白须公”“红帝公”，建祠奉祀。

中国的海神崇拜由来已久，《山海经》中就记载了四海之神与四海龙王，民间也早就有风神水怪祭祀。然而，对百姓来说，这些自然神威严有余，慈爱不足，只能敬而远之。于是，他们就在心中盼望一位更接地气的神来佑护航行，拯救海难。

通远王坐像（中）。（陈英杰 摄）
The sitting statue of King Tongyuan (middle), the sea deity. (Photo by Chen Yingjie)

Belief in King Tongyuan, the Sea Deity

Originating during the Tang and Song dynasties, King Tongyuan is the first generation of sea god in China.

King Tongyuan, whose secular name is Li Yuanpu, was a native of Sichuan and became an imperial scholar between 742 and 756. He was the author of the book *Sound of the Divine* and once served as the assistant regiment commander of Yunnan militia. Later, in order to escape from the war, he abandoned his official position and lived in seclusion. When he travelled to Leshan Mountain at the junction of Nan'an and Yongchun in Quanzhou, he built a house and settled down. He spent the following twenty or more years practicing Dharma here before he became an immortal whom the villagers honored as King of Leshan Mountain.

Legend has it that after his ascension to immortality, he became an inspirational role model of the Tang and Song dynasties, busying using his divine power to help the people. Stories of his could be found in *Local Gazetteer of Nan'an County, Vol. 2 Geography*, "Between 860 and 874, a monk went to Leshan Mountain in Yongchun to look for wood to build a temple, and on his way, he met an old man who showed him the way...The old man turned out to be the deity, King of Leshan Mountain, so he built a temple to worship him. Whenever there were floods, droughts, epidemics or when people were going on a voyage, they would pray for his protection and blessings. And all their prayers were answered." Grateful to his mighty acts, people called him White Beard God or Red God and built temples to worship him.

The worship of sea gods enjoys a long history in China. Four gods of the sea and four dragon kings were recorded in the earliest cultural and geographical record in China, *The Classic of Mountains and Seas*, and the worship of wind gods and water monsters has long been practiced. However, for common people, these gods of nature were more dignified than loving, so they were always kept at a respectful distance. Therefore, a more easygoing god was expected to escort common people and protect them from ship wrecks.

来了！那个能调节大海呼吸脉搏的神一样的男人！宋政和四年（1114），朝廷为其立庙，赐额“昭惠”，后封“通远王”“广福王”“善利王”“显济王”爵号，晋为“福佑帝君”。“乐山白衣叟”的海神地位正式确立。

之后，通远王由南安五台山昭惠庙分身到海边金鸡港九日山昭惠庙，神通广大，能保佑“风息涛平”，完全是一尊泉州海外交通贸易的海上保护神了。九日山石刻记载，宋时，泉州官府每年都到九日山昭惠庙举行冬夏两次声势浩大的祈风祭祀典礼，碑文有“舶司岁两祈风于通远王庙”的记述，见证海神通远王崇祀盛况。

这在当时属于非常拉风的事情，地方州郡一把手偕市舶司官员向海祈风以佑贸易之事，在古代中国，仅泉州有此俗，而地方史官把此事像年鉴一样刻在山中临海神庙的摩崖石壁上，也算是前无古人。整个大宋朝，此风在泉州延绵不绝。由此，从庙堂之高到江湖之远，无人不为海上丝绸之路的风正帆悬、财通四海而点赞。其中，人们致以最高敬意的，自然是通远王。

有实力才有魅力，崇高的地位来自非凡的神力。通远王信俗历史悠久，世代传承，识家早就发现，其对研究泉州海外交通史和海上丝绸之路史迹具有重大意义。在宋元中国的世界海洋商贸中心，通远王信俗包含了多重文化密码，汇通了不同地区、不同民族交融绸缪的共同文化表征，因此也得以在中国台港澳地区和韩国、日本及东南亚一些国家广泛传播，其在海内外的影响力，可谓至深至远。

此境通远，比永远更远；故乡有月，比他乡更圆。海上风云，似已尘埃落定；彼岸乡愁，此际依旧涛声。和泪向海，挥别昨夜星辰，征帆归来之际，容我喊一声——

“王者，何时归来？”

昭惠庙举办通远王诞辰祭祀活动。（苏德辉 摄）
A sacrificial rite to the birthday of King Tongyuan held in Zhaohui Temple. (Photo by Su Dehui)

Here he came, the deity which could regulate the pulse of the sea. In 1114, the position of the man in white from Leshan Mountain as a sea god was officially established when the imperial court built a temple named Zhaohui for him, bestowing him titles such as King Tongyuan, King Guangfu, King Shanli, King Xianji, and even Emperor Fuyou.

Afterwards, King Tongyuan was branched out from Zhaohui Temple in Wutai Mountain in Nan'an to Zhaohui Temple in Jiuri Mountain by Jinji Port, where he was completely transformed to a sea protector of the overseas traffic and trade of Quanzhou with his great divine power. Every summer and winter in the Song Dynasty, the local government of Quanzhou would hold ritual ceremonies at Zhaohui Temple in Jiuri Mountain praying for favorable winds to aid voyages. Records of these ceremonies can be found on the wind-praying cliff inscriptions in Jiuri Mountain.

In those days, it was a very popular event when the local governor of Quanzhou, together with officials of the Maritime Trade Office, prayed for favorable winds to aid voyages and trades. And this custom, unique to Quanzhou, continued throughout the Song Dynasty and was widely accepted by both the court and the common people. Of course, the highest respect went, as always, to the sea deity, King Tongyuan. What was also unprecedented was that the local historians carved records of the events on the cliff stones near Zhaohui Temple like a yearbook.

The divine power brings forth great charisma. The Belief in King Tongyuan has a long history and has been passed down from generation to generation. Visionary scholars have long since discovered that it is of great significance to the study of Quanzhou's overseas transportation history and the historical sites and relics of the Maritime Silk Road. In Quanzhou, the Emporium of the World in Song-Yuan China, the Belief in King Tongyuan and related customs contain multiple cultural codes, integrating the common cultural representations of different regions and nationalities. It has, therefore, been widely spread in regions like Taiwan, Hong Kong and Macao and countries like South Korea, Japan and some Southeast Asian ones.

There is nothing more powerful than faith. The Belief in King Tongyuan links the hearts of people not only on both sides of the Taiwan Strait but also around the world.

图书在版编目（CIP）数据

流风遗韵：宋元泉州非遗的承与传：汉英对照 / 中共泉州市委宣传部编．--福州：福建人民出版社，2024.6（2025.3重印）
（世遗之城：泉州）
ISBN 978-7-211-09039-6

Ⅰ.①流… Ⅱ. ①中… Ⅲ.①非物质文化遗产—泉州—宋元时期—汉、英 Ⅳ.①G127.573

中国国家版本馆 CIP 数据核字（2023）第 078990 号

流风遗韵——宋元泉州非遗的承与传
LIUFENG YIYUN——SONGYUAN QUANZHOU FEIYI DE CHENG YU CHUAN

特约撰稿：谢万智　姚　伟
翻　　译：黄娟娟
责任编辑：孙　颖
美术编辑：陈培亮
责任校对：李雪莹
装帧设计：雅昌（上海）设计中心
出版发行：福建人民出版社　　电　　话：0591-87533169(发行部)
网　　址：http://www.fjpph.com　　电子邮箱：fjpph7211@126.com
地　　址：福州市东水路 76 号　　邮政编码：350001
经　　销：福建新华发行（集团）有限责任公司
印　　刷：雅昌文化（集团）有限公司
地　　址：深圳市南山区深云路 19 号
电　　话：0755-86083235
开　　本：787 毫米×1092 毫米　1/16
印　　张：11.5
字　　数：294 千字
版　　次：2024 年 6 月第 1 版
印　　次：2025 年 3 月第 2 次印刷
书　　号：ISBN 978-7-211-09039-6
定　　价：58.00 元